Nomadology:
The War Machine

Deleuze and Guattari

D1570654

FOREIGN AGENTS SERIES

Jim Fleming and Sylvere Lotringer, Series Editors

Nomadology:
The War Machine

Gilles Deleuze
and
Félix Guattari

Translated by Brian Massumi

Originally published in French
as "Traité de nomadologie:
La machine de guerre,"
in *Mille Plateaux*, Paris,
Editions de Minuit.

This translation published by
arrangement with University
of Minnesota Press.
We acknowledge for translation
assistance the French Ministry
of Culture and the National
Endowment for the Humanities.
We acknowledge for publication
assistance the New York State
Council on the Arts.

Nomadology:
The War Machine

Axiom 1: The war machine is exterior to the State apparatus.

Proposition 1: This exteriority is first attested to in mythology, epic, drama and games.

Georges Dumézil, in his definitive analyses of Indo-European mythology, has shown that political sovereignty, or domination, has two heads: the magician-king and the jurist-priest. Rex and flamen, raj and Brahman, Romulus and Numa, Varuna and Mitra, the despot and the legislator, the binder and the organizer. Undoubtedly, these two poles stand in opposition term by term, as the obscure and the clear, the violent and the calm, the quick and the weighty, the fearsome and the regulated, the "bond" and the "pact," etc.[1] But their opposition is only relative; they function as a pair, in alternation, as though they expressed a division of the One or constituted in themselves a sovereign unity. "At once antithetical and complementary, necessary to one another and consequently without hostility, lacking a mythology of conflict: a specification on any one level automatically calls forth a homologous specification on another. The two together exhaust the field of the function." They are the principal elements of a State apparatus that proceeds by a One-Two, distributes binary distinctions and forms a milieu of interiority. It is a double articulation that makes the State apparatus into a *stratum*.

It will be noted that war is not contained within this apparatus. *Either* the State has at its disposal a violence that is not channelled through war—either it uses policemen and jailers in place of warriors, has no arms and no need of them, operates through immediate, magical capture, "seizes" and "binds," preventing all combat—*or*, the State acquires an army, but in a way that presupposes a juridical integration of war and the organization of a military function.[2] As for the war machine in itself, it seems to be irreducible to the State apparatus, to be outside its sovereignty and prior to its law: it comes from elsewhere. *Indra, the warrior god, is in opposition to Varuna no less than to Mitra.*[3] He can no more be reduced to one or the other than can he constitute a third of their kind. Rather, he is like a pure and immeasurable multiplicity, the pack, an irruption of the ephemeral and the power of metamorphosis. *He unties the bond just as he betrays the pact*. He brings a *furor* to bear against sovereignty, a celerity against gravity, secrecy against the public, a power *(puissance)* against sovereignty, a machine against the apparatus. He bears witness to another kind of justice, one of incomprehensible cruelty at times, but at others of unequaled pity as well (because he unties bonds . . .).[4] He bears witness, above all, to other relations with women, with animals, because he sees all things in relations of *becoming,* rather than implementing binary distributions between "states": a veritable becoming-animal of the warrior, a becoming-woman, which lies outside dualities of terms as well as correspondences between relations. In every respect, the war machine is of another species, another nature, another origin than the State apparatus.

Let us take a limited example, and compare the war machine and the State apparatus in the context of the theory of games. Let us take chess and Go, from the standpoint of the game pieces, the relations between the pieces and the space involved. Chess is a game of State, or of the court: the emperor of China played it. Chess pieces are coded; they have an internal nature and intrinsic properties, from which their movements, situations and confrontations derive. They have qualities; a knight remains a knight, a pawn a pawn, a bishop a bishop. Each is like a subject of the statement endowed with a relative power, and these relative powers combine in a subject of enunciation, the chess player himself or the game's form of interiority. Go pieces, in contrast, are pellets, disks, simple arithmetic units, and have only an anonymous, collective or third person function: "It" makes a move. "It" could be a man, a woman, a louse, an elephant.

Go pieces are elements of a nonsubjectified machine assemblage with no intrinsic properties, but only situational ones. Thus the relations are very different in the two cases. Within their milieu of interiority, chess pieces entertain biunique relations with one another, and with the adversary's pieces: their functioning is structural. On the other hand, a Go piece has only a milieu of exteriority, or extrinsic relations with nebulas or constellations, according to which it fulfills functions of insertion or situation, such as bordering, encircling, shattering. All by itself, a Go piece can destroy an entire constellation synchronically; a chess piece cannot (or can do so diachronically only).

Chess is indeed a war, but an institutionalized, regulated, coded war, with a front, a rear, battles. But what is proper to Go is war without battle lines, with neither confrontation nor retreat, without battles even: pure strategy, while chess is a semiology. Finally, the space is not at all the same: in chess, it is a question of arranging a closed space for oneself, thus of going from one point to another, of occupying the maximum number of squares with the minimum number of pieces. In Go, it is a question of arraying oneself in an open space, of holding space, of maintaining the possibility of springing up at any point: the movement is not from one point to another, but becomes perpetual, without aim or destination, without departure or arrival. The "smooth" space of Go, as against the "striated" space of chess. The *nomos* of Go against the State of chess, *nomos* against *polis*. The difference is that chess codes and decodes space, while Go proceeds altogether differently territorializing or deterritorializing it (make the outside a territory in space; consolidate that territory by the construction of a second, adjacent territory; deterritorialize the enemy by shattering his territory from within; deterritorialize oneself by renouncing, by going elsewhere . . .). Another justice, another movement, another space-time.

"They come like fate, without reason, consideration, or pretext . . ." "In some way that is incomprehensible they have pushed right into the capital. At any rate, here they are; it seems that every morning there are more of them."[5] Luc de Heusch analyzes a Bantu myth that leads us to the same schema: Nkongolo, an indigenous emperor and administrator of public works, a man of the public and a man of the police, gives his half-sisters to the hunter Mbidi, who assists him, and then leaves. Mbidi's son, a man of secrecy, joins up with his father, only to return from the outside with that inconceivable thing, an army. He kills Nkongolo, and proceeds to build a new State . . .[6] "Between" the magical-despotic State and the juridical State containing a military institution, we see the flash of the war machine, arriving from without.

From the standpoint of the State, the originality of the man of war, his eccentricity, necessarily appears in a negative form: stupidity, deformity, madness, illegitimacy, usurpation, sin . . . Dumézil analyzes the three "sins" of the warrior in the Indo-European tradition: against the king, against the priest, against the laws originating in the State (for example, a sexual transgression that compromises the distribution of men and women, or even a betrayal of the laws of war as instituted by the State).[7] The warrior is in the position of betraying everything, including the function of the military, *or* of understanding nothing. It happens that historians, both bourgeois and Soviet, will follow this negative tradition and explain how Genghis Khan understood nothing: he "didn't understand" the phenomenon of the city. An easy thing to say. The problem is that the exteriority of the war machine in relation to the State apparatus is everywhere apparent, but remains difficult to conceptualize. It is not enough to affirm that the war machine is external to the apparatus. It is necessary to reach the point of conceiving the war machine as itself a pure form of exteriority, whereas the State apparatus constitutes the form of interiority we habitually take as a model, or according to which we are in the habit of thinking.

What complicates everything is that this extrinsic power of the war machine tends, under certain circumstances, to become confused with one of the two heads of the State apparatus. Sometimes it is confused with the magic violence of the State, at other times with the State's military institution. For instance, the war machine invents speed and secrecy; but there is all the same a certain speed and a certain secrecy that pertain to the State, relatively, secondarily. So there is a great danger of identifying the structural relation between the two poles of political sovereignty, and the dynamic interrelation of these two poles, with the power *(puissance)* of war. Dumézil cites the lineage of the Roman kings: there is a Romulus-Numa relation that recurs throughout a series, with variants and an alternation between these two types of equally legitimate rulers; but there is also a relation with an "evil king," Tullus Hostilius, Tarquinus the Proud, an upsurge of the warrior as a disquieting and illegitimate character.[8] Shakespeare's kings could also be invoked: even violence, murders and perversion do not prevent the State lineage from producing "good" kings; but a disquieting character like Richard III slips in, announcing from the outset his intention to reinvent a war machine and impose its line (deformed, deceitful and traiterous, he claims a "secret close intent"[9] totally different from the conquest of State power, and another—an *other*—relation with women).

In short, whenever the irruption of war power is confused with the line of State domination, everything becomes muddled; the war machine can then be understood only through the categories of the negative, since nothing is left that remains outside the State. But, returned to its milieu of exteriority, the war machine is seen to be of another species, of another nature, of another origin. One would have to say that it is located between the two heads of the State, between the two articulations, and that it is necessary in order to pass from one to the other. But "between" the two, in that instant, even ephemeral, if only a flash, it proclaims its own irreducibility. *The State has no war machine of its own;* it can only appropriate one in the form of a military institution, one that will always cause it problems. This explains the mistrust States have towards their military institutions, to the extent that the State inherits an extrinsic war machine. Carl von Clausewitz has a general sense of this situation when he treats the flow of absolute war as an Idea which States partially appropriate according to their political needs, and in relation to which they are more or less good "conductors."[10]

Trapped between the two poles of political sovereignty, the man of war seems outmoded, condemned, without a future, reduced to his own fury, which he turns against himself. The descendants of Hercules, Achilles, then Ajax, have enough strength left to proclaim their independence from Agamenmon, a man of the old State. But they are powerless when it comes to Ulysses, a man of the nascent modern State, the first man of the modern State. And it is Ulysses who inherits Achilles' arms, only to convert them to other uses, submitting them to the laws of the State—not Ajax, who is condemned by the goddess he defied and against whom he sinned.[11] No one has portrayed the situation of the man of war, at once eccentric and condemned, better than Kleist. In *Penthesileia*, Achilles is already separated from his power (*puissance*): the war machine has passed over to the Amazons, a Stateless woman-people whose justice, religion, and loves are organized uniquely in a war mode. Descendents of the Scythians, the Amazons spring forth like lightning, "between" the two States, the Greek and the Trojan. They sweep away everything in their path. Achilles is brought before his double, Penthesileia. And in his ambiguous struggle, Achilles is unable to prevent himself from marrying the war machine, or from loving Penthesileia, and thus from betraying Agamemnon and Ulysses at the same time. Nevertheless, he already belongs enough to the Greek State that Penthesileia, for her part, cannot enter the passional relation of war with him without herself betraying the collective law of her people, the law of the pack that prohibits "choosing" the enemy and entering into one-to-one relationships or binary distinctions.

Throughout his work, Kleist celebrates the war machine, setting it against the State apparatus in a struggle that is lost from the start. Doubtless Arminius heralds a Germanic war machine that breaks with the imperial order of alliances and armies, and stands forever opposed to the Roman State. But the Prince of Homburg lives only in a dream, and stands condemned for having reached victory in disobedience of the law of the State. As for Kohlhaas, his war machine can no longer be anything more than banditry. Is it the destiny of the war machine, when the State triumphs, to be caught in this alternative: either to be nothing more than the disciplined, military organ of the State apparatus, *or to turn against itself,* to become a double suicide machine for a solitary man and a solitary woman? Goethe and Hegel, State thinkers both, see Kleist as a monster, and Kleist has lost from the start. Why is it, then, that the most uncanny modernity lies with him? It is because the elements of his work are secrecy, speed and affect.[12] And in Kleist the secret is no longer a content held within a form of interiority; rather, it becomes a form, identified with the form of exteriority which is always external to itself. Similarly, feelings become uprooted from the interiority of a "subject," to be projected violently outward into a milieu of pure exteriority that lends them an incredible velocity, a catapulting force: love or hate, they are no longer feelings, but affects. And these affects are so many instances of the becoming-woman, the becoming-animal of the warrior (the bear, she-dogs). Affects transpierce the body like arrows, they are weapons of war. The deterritorialization velocity of affect. Even dreams (Homburg's, Pentheseleia's) are externalized, by a system of relays and plug-ins, extrinsic linkages belonging to the war machine. Broken rings.

This element of exteriority—which dominates everything, which Kleist invents in literature, which he is the first to invent—will give time a new rhythm: an endless succession of catatonic episodes or fainting spells, and flashes or rushes. Catatonia is: "this affect is too strong for me," and a flash is: "the power of this affect sweeps me away," so that the Self *(Moi)* is now nothing more than a character whose actions and emotions are desubjectified, perhaps even to the point of death. Such is Kleist's personal formula: a succession of flights of madness and catatonic freezes in which no subjective interiority remains. There is much of the East in Kleist: the Japanese fighter, interminably still, who then makes a move too quick to see. The Go player. Many things in modern art come from Kleist. Goethe and Hegel are old men next to Kleist. Could it be that it is at the moment the war machine ceases to exist, conquered by the State, that it displays to the utmost its irreducibility, that it scatters into thinking, loving, dying, or creating machines which have at their disposal vital or revolutionary powers capable of challenging the conquering State? Is the war machine already overtaken, condemned, appropriated as part of the same process whereby it takes on new forms, undergoes a metamorphosis, affirms its irreducibility and exteriority, and deploys that milieu of pure exteriority which the Occidental man of the State, or the Occidental thinker, never ceases to reduce to something other than itself?

Problem 1: Is there a way of warding off the formation of a state apparatus (or its equivalents in a group)?

Proposition 2: The exteriority of the war machine is also attested to by ethnology (a tribute to the memory of Pierre Clastres).

Primitive, segmentary societies have often been defined as societies without a State, meaning societies in which distinct organs of power do not appear. But the conclusion has been that these societies did not reach the degree of economic development, or the level of political differentiation, that would make the formation of the State apparatus both possible and inevitable: the implication is that primitive people "don't understand" so complex an apparatus. The prime interest in Pierre Clastres' theories is his break with this evolutionist postulate. Not only does he doubt that the State is the product of an ascribable economic development, but he asks if it is not a potential concern of primitive societies to ward off or avert that monster they supposedly do not understand. Warding off the formation of a State apparatus, making such a formation impossible, would be the objective of a certain number of primitive social mechanisms, even if they are not consciously understood as such. To be sure, primitive societies have *chiefs*. But the State is not defined by the existence of chiefs; it is defined by the perpetuation or conservation of organs of power. The concern of the State is to conserve. Special institutions are thus necessary to enable a chief to become a man of State, but diffuse, collective mechanisms are just as necessary to prevent a chief from becoming one. Mechanisms for warding off, preventive mechanisms, are a part of chieftainship, and keep an apparatus distinct from the social body from crystallizing. Clastres describes the situation of the chief, who has no instituted weapon other than his prestige, no other means of persuasion, no other rule than his sense of the group's desires. The chief is more like a leader or a star than a man of power, and is always in danger of being disavowed, abandoned by his people.

But Clastres goes further, identifying *war* in primitive societies as the surest mechanism directed against the formation of the State: war maintains the dispersal and segmentarity of groups, and the warrior himself is caught in the process of accumulating exploits, a process which leads him on to solitude and a prestigious death, but without power.[13] Clastres can thus invoke natural Law while reversing its principal proposition: just as Hobbes saw clearly that *the State was against war, so war is against the State,* and makes it impossible. It should not be concluded that war is a state of nature, but rather that it is the mode of a social state that wards off and prevents the State. Primitive war does not produce the State any more than it derives from it. And it is no more explained by exchange than it is by the State: far from deriving from exchange, even as a sanction for its failure, war is what limits exchanges, maintains them in the framework of "alliances," what prevents them from becoming a State factor, from fusing groups together.

The importance of this thesis is first of all to draw attention to collective mechanisms of inhibition. These mechanisms may be subtle, and function as micromechanisms. This is easily seen in certain band or pack phenomena. For example, in relation to gangs of street children in Bogotá, Jacques Meunier cites three ways in which the leader is prevented from acquiring stable power: the members of the band meet and undertake their theft activity in common, with collective sharing of the loot, but they disperse, and do not remain together to eat or sleep; also, and especially, each member of the band is paired off with one, two, or three other members, so if he has a disagreement with the leader, he will not leave alone, but will take along his allies, whose combined departure will threaten to break up the entire gang; finally, there is a diffuse age limit such that towards age fifteen a member is inevitably induced to quit the gang.[14] These mechanisms he understood without renouncing the evolutionist vision that sees bands or packs as a rudimentary, less organized social form. Even in bands of animals, leadership is a complex mechanism that does not act to promote the strongest, but rather inhibits the installation of stable powers, in favor of a web of immanent relations.[15] One could just as easily compare the form "high society life" to the form "sociability" among the most highly evolved men and women: high society groups are similar to gangs, and operate by the diffusion of prestige rather than by reference to centers of power, as in social groupings (Proust clearly showed this noncorrespondence of high society values and social values). Eugène Sue, a man of high society and a dandy, whom legitimists reproached for frequenting the Orléans family, used to say: "I'm not on the side of the family, I side with the pack." Packs, bands, are groups of the rhizome type, as opposed to the arborescent type which centers around organs of power. That is why bands in general, even those engaged in banditry or high society life, are metamorphoses of a war machine that differs formally from all State apparatuses or their equivalents, which, on the contrary, structure centralized societies. One certainly would not say that discipline is what defines a war machine: discipline becomes the charac- teristic required of armies when the State appropriates them. But the war machine answers to other rules. We are of course not saying that they are better, only that they animate a fundamental indiscipline of the warrior, a ques- tioning of hierarchy, perpetual blackmailing by aban- donment or betrayal, and a very volatile sense of honor, all of which, once again, impedes the formation of the State.

But why is it that this argument fails to convince us entirely? We go along with Clastres when he demon- strates that the State is explained neither by a develop- ment of productive forces, nor by a differentiation of political forces. It is the State, on the contrary, that makes possible the undertaking of large-scale projects, the constitution of surpluses, and the organization of the corresponding public functions. It is the State that makes possible the distinction between governors and governed. We do not see how the State can be explained by what it presupposes, even with recourse to dialectics. The State does seem to rise up in a single stroke, in an imperial form, and does not depend on progressive factors. Its on-the-spot emergence is like a stroke of genius, the birth of Athena.

We also follow Clastres when he shows how the war machine is directed against the State, either against potential States whose formation it wards off in advance, or against actual States whose destruction it purposes. No doubt the war machine is realized more completely in the "barbaric" assemblages of nomadic warriors than in the "savage" assemblages of primitive societies. In any case, it is out of the question that the State could be the result of a war in which the conquerors imposed through their victory a new law on the vanquished, since the organization of the war machine is directed against the State-form, actual or virtual. The State is no better accounted for as a result of war than by a progression of economic or political forces. This is where Clastres locates the break: between "primitive" counter-State societies and "monstrous" State-societies whose formation it is no longer possible to explain. Clastres is fascinated by the problem of "voluntary servitude," in the manner of La Boétie: in what way did people want or desire servitude, which most certainly did not come to them as the outcome of an involuntary and unfortunate war? They did, after all, have counter-State mechanisms at their disposal: so how and why the State? Why did the State triumph?

It is as if the more deeply he delved into the problem, the more Pierre Clastres deprived himself of the means of resolving it.[16] He tended to make primitive societies a hypostasis, a self-sufficient entity (he insisted heavily on this point). He made their formal exteriority into a real independence. In so doing, he remained an evolutionist, and posited a state of nature. Only this state of nature was, according to him, a fully social reality instead of a pure concept, and the evolution was a sudden mutation instead of a development. For on the one hand, the State arose in a single stroke, fully formed; on the other, the counter-State societies used very specific mechanisms to ward it off, to prevent it from arising. We believe that these two propositions are valid, but that their inter-linkage is flawed. There is an old scenario: "from clans to empires," or "from bands to kingdoms . . ." But nothing says that this constitutes an evolution, since bands and clans are no less organized than empire-kingdoms. We will never leave the evolution hypothesis behind by creating a break between the two terms, that is, by endowing bands with self-sufficiency and the State with an emergence all the more miraculous and monstrous.

We are compelled to say that there has always been a State, quite perfect, quite complete. The more discoveries archeologists make, the more empires they uncover. The hypothesis of the *Urstaat* seems to be verified: "the State clearly dates back to the most remote ages of humanity." It is hard to imagine primitive societies that would not have been in contact with imperial States, at the periphery or in poorly controlled areas. But of greater importance is the inverse hypothesis: that the State itself has always been in a relation with an outside, and is inconceivable independent of that relationship. The law of the State is not the law of All or Nothing (State-societies *or* counter-State societies), but that of interior and exterior. The State is sovereignty. But sovereignty only reigns over what it is capable of internalizing, of appropriating locally. Not only is there no universal State, but the outside of States cannot be reduced to "foreign policy," that is to a set of relations among States. The outside appears simultaneously in two directions: huge world-wide machines branched out over the entire *ecumenon* at any given moment, which enjoy a large measure of autonomy in relation to the States (for example, commercial organization of the "multinational" type, or industrial complexes, or even religious formations like Christianity, Islam, certain prophetic or messianic movements, etc.); but also the local mechanisms of bands, margins, minorities, which continue to affirm the rights of segmentary societies in opposition to the organs of State power. The modern world can provide us today with particularly well-developed images of these two directions, in the way of worldwide ecumenical machines, but also a neoprimitivism, a new tribal society as Marshall McLuhan describes it. These directions are equally present in all social fields, in all periods. It even happens that they become partially merged. For example, a commercial organization is also a band of pillage, or piracy, for part of its course and in many of its activities; or it is in bands that a religious formation begins to operate. What becomes clear is that bands, no less than worldwide organizations, imply a form irreducible to the State, and that this exteriority necessarily presents itself as that of a diffuse and polymorphous war machine. It is a *nomos* very different from the "law."

The State-form, as a form of interiority, has a tendency to reproduce itself, remaining identical to itself across its variations and easily recognizable within the limits of its poles, always seeking public recognition (there is no masked State). But the war machine's form of exteriority is such that it exists only in its own metamorphoses; it exists in an industrial innovation as well as in a technological invention, in a commercial circuit as well as in a religious creation, in all the flows and currents that only secondarily allow themselves to be appropriated by the State. It is not in terms of independence, but of coexistence and competition *in a perpetual field of interaction,* that we must conceive of exteriority and interiority, war machines of metamorphosis and State apparatuses of identity, bands and kingdoms, megamachines and empires. The same field circumscribes its interiority in States, but describes its exteriority in what escapes States or stands against States.

> *Proposition 3: The exteriority of the war machine is also attested to by epistemology, which intimates the existence and perpetuation of a "nomad" or "minor science."*

There is a kind of science, or treatment of science, that seems very difficult to classify, the history of which is even difficult to follow. What we are referring to are not "technologies" in the usual sense of the term. But neither are they "sciences" in the royal or legal sense established by history. According to a recent book by Michel Serres, the trace of it can be found both in the atomic physics of Democritus and Lucretius, and in the geometry of Archimedes.[17] The characteristics of this kind of eccentric science would seem to be the following:

1) First of all, it uses a hydraulic model, rather than constituting a theory of solids that treats fluids as a special case; ancient atomism is inseparable from flows, flux is reality itself, or consistency.

2) The model in question is one of becoming and heterogeneity, as opposed to the stable, the eternal, the identical, the constant. It is a "paradox" to make becoming itself a model, and no longer a secondary characteristic, a copy; in the *Timaeus,* Plato raises this possibility, but only in order to exclude it and conjure it away in the name of royal science. By contrast, in atomism, just such a model of heterogeneity, and of passage or becoming in the heterogeneous, is furnished by the famed declination of the atom. The *clinamen,* as the minimum angle, has meaning only between a straight line and a curve, the curve and its tangent, and constitutes the original curvature of the movement of the atom. The clinamen is the smallest angle by which an atom deviates from a straight path. It is a passage to the limit, an exhaustion, a paradoxical "exhaustive" model. The same applies for Archimedean geometry, in which the straight line, defined as "the shortest path between two points," is just a way of defining the length of a curve in a predifferential calculus.

3) One no longer goes from the straight line to its parallels, in a lamellar or laminar flow, but from a curvilinear declination to the formation of spirals and vortices on an inclined plane: the greatest slope for the smallest angle. From *turba* to *turbo*: in other words from bands or packs of atoms to the great vortical organizations. The model is a vortical one; it operates in an open space throughout which thing-flows are distributed, rather than plotting out a closed space for linear and solid things. It is the difference between a *smooth* (vectorial, projective or topological) space and a *striated* (metric) space: in the first case "space is occupied without being counted," while in the second case "space is counted in

order to be occupied."[18]

4) Finally, the model is problematic, instead of theorematic: figures are considered only from the point of view of the *affections* that befall them: sections, ablations, adjunctions, projections. One does not proceed by specific differences from a genus to its species, nor by deduction from a stable essence to the properties deriving from it, but from a problem to the accidents that condition and resolve it. This involves all manner of deformations, transmutations, passages to the limit, operations in which each figure designates an "event" much more than an essence; the square no longer exists independently of a quadrature, the cube of a cubature, the straight line of a rectification. Whereas the theorem is of the rational order *(de l'ordre des raisons)*, the problem is affective, and is inseparable from the metamorphoses, generations and creations within science itself. Despite what Gabriel Marcel may say, the problem is not an "obstacle," it is the surpassing of the obstacle, a projection, in other words a war machine. All that movement is what royal science is striving to limit when it reduces as much as possible the range of the "problem-element" and subordinates it to the "theorem-element."[19]

This Archimedean science, or this conception of science, is bound up in an essential way with the war machine: the *problemata* are the war machine itself, and are inseparable from the inclined planes, passages to the limit, vortices and projections. It would seem that the war machine is projected into an abstract knowledge formally different from the one that doubles the State apparatus. It would seem that an entire nomad science develops eccentrically, one that is very different from the royal or imperial sciences. Furthermore, this nomad science is constantly being "barred," inhibited or banned by the demands and conditions of State science. Archimedes, vanquished by the Roman State, becomes a symbol.[20] The fact is that the two kinds of science have different modes of formalization, and State science is constantly imposing its form of sovereignty on the inventions of nomad science. What State science retains of nomad science is only what it can appropriate; it turns what remains into a set of strictly limited formulas without any real scientific status, or else simply represses and bans it. It is as if the "savant" of nomad science were caught between a rock and a hard place, between the war machine that nourishes and inspires him and the State that imposes upon him a rational order *(ordre des raisons)*.

The figure of the *engineer* (in particular the military engineer), with all its ambivalence, is illustrative of this situation. Most significant are perhaps the borderline phenomena where nomad science exerts pressure on State science, and, conversely, where State science appropriates and transforms the elements of nomad science. This is true of the art of encampments, and inclined planes: the State does not appropriate this dimension of the war machine without submitting it to civil and metric rules that strictly limit, control, localize nomad science, and without keeping it from having repercussions throughout the social field (in this respect, Vauban is like a repeat of Archimedes, and suffers an analogous defeat). It is true of descriptive and projective geometry, which royal science would like to turn into a mere practical dependency of analytical, or so-called "higher," geometry (thus the ambiguous situation of Monge and Poncelet as "savants"[21]). It is also true of differential calculus: for a long time, it had only parascientific status, it was labeled a "gothic hypothesis," royal science only accorded it the value of a convenient convention or a well-founded fiction; the great State mathematicians did their best to improve its status, but precisely on the condition that all the dynamic, nomadic notions—such as becoming, heterogeneity, infinitesimal, passage to the limit, continuous variation, etc.—be eliminated, and that civil, static and ordinal rules be imposed upon it (Carnot's ambiguous position in this respect). Finally, it is true of the hydraulic model: for it is certain that the State itself needs a hydraulic science (there is no going back on Wittfogel's theses on the importance of large-scale waterworks for an empire). But it needs it in a very different form, because the State needs to subordinate hydraulic force to conduits, pipes, embankments which prevent turbulence, which constrain movement to go from one point to another, and space itself to be striated and measured, which makes the fluid depend on the solid, and flows proceed by parallel, laminar layers. The hydraulic model of nomad science and the war machine, on the other hand, consists in being distributed by turbulence across a smooth space, in producing a movement that holds space and simultaneously affects all of its points, instead of being held by space in a local movement from one specified point to another.[22] Democritus, Menaechmus, Archimedes, Vauban, Desargues, Bernoulli, Monge, Carnot, Poncelet, Perronet, etc.: in each case a monograph would be necessary to take into account the special situation of these savants whom State science used only after restraining or disciplining them, after repressing their social or political conceptions.

The sea as a smooth space is a specific problem of the

war machine. As Virilio shows, it is at sea that the problem of the *fleet in being* is posed, in other words the task of occupying an open space with a vortical movement that can rise up at any point. In this respect, the recent studies on rhythm, on the origin of that notion, do not seem entirely convincing. For we are told that rhythm has nothing to do with the movement of waves, but that it designates "form" in general, and more specifically the form of a "measured, cadenced" movement.[23] Rhythm and measure, however, are always distinct. And though the atomist, Democritus, is one of the authors who speak of rhythm in the sense of form, it should not be forgotten that he does so under very precise conditions of fluctuation, and that the forms made by atoms constitute first of all large, nonmetric aggregates, smooth spaces such as the air, the sea or even the earth *(magnae res)*. There is indeed such a thing as measured, cadensed rhythm, relating to the coursing of a river between its banks or to the form of a striated space; but there is also a rhythm without measure, which relates to the upswell of a flow, in other words to the manner in which a fluid occupies a smooth space.

This opposition, or rather this tension-limit between the two kinds of science—nomad, war-machine science and royal, State science—reappears at different moments, on different levels. The work of Anne Querrien enables us to identify two of these moments; one is the construction of Gothic cathedrals in the twelfth century, the other the construction of bridges in the eighteenth and nineteenth centuries.[24] Gothic architecture is indeed inseparable from a will to build churches longer and taller than the Romanesque churches. Ever farther, ever higher . . . But this difference is not simply quantitative, it marks a qualitative change: the static relation, form-matter, tends to fade into the background in favor of a dynamic relation, material-forces. It is the cutting of the stone that turns it into material capable of holding and coordinating forces of thrust, and of constructing ever higher and longer vaults. The vault is no longer a form, but the line of continuous variation of the stones. It is as if Gothic conquered a smooth space, while Romanesque remained partially within a striated space (where the vault depends on the juxtaposition of parallel pillars). But stone-cutting is inseparable from on the one hand a plane of projection at ground level, which functions as a plane limit, and on the other hand a series of successive approximations (squaring), or variable shapings of voluminous stones. Of course, it was to the theorematic science of Euclid that one turned in order to find a foundation for the enterprise: mathematical figures and equations were thought to be the intelligible form capable of organizing surfaces and volumes. But according to the legend, Bernard de Clairvaux quickly abandoned the effort as too "difficult," appealing to the specificity of an operative, Archimedean geometry, a projective and descriptive geometry defined as a minor science, more a mathegraphy than a matheology. His journeyman, the monk-mason Garin de Troyes, speaks of an operative logic of movement enabling the "initiate" to trace, then hew the volumes "in penetration in space," to make it so that "the cutting-line propels the equation" *(le trait pousse le chiffre).*[25] One does not represent, one engenders and traverses. This science is characterized less by the absence of equations than by the very different role they play: instead of being good forms absolutely which organize matter, they are "generated" as "forces of thrust" *(poussées)* by the material, in a qualitative calculus of the optimum.

This whole current of Archimedean geometry was taken to its highest expression, but was also brought to a temporary standstill, with the remarkable seventeenth-century mathematician, Desargues. Like most of his kind, Desargues wrote little; he nevertheless exerted a great influence through his actions, and left outlines, rough drafts, and projects, all centered on problem-events: "Lamentations," "draft project for the cutting of stones," "draft project for grappling with the events of the encounters of a cone and a plane. . . ." Desargues, however, was condemned by the *parlement* of Paris, opposed by the king's secretary; his practices of perspective were banned.[26] Royal, or State, science only tolerates and appropriates stone-cutting by means of *templates* (the opposite of squaring), under conditions which restore the primacy of the fixed model of form, mathematical figures and measurement. Royal science only tolerates and appropriates perspective if it is static, subjected to a central black hole divesting it of its heuristic and ambulatory capacities. But the adventure, or event, of Desargues is the same as had already been produced among the Gothic "journeymen" on a collective level. For not only did the Church, in its imperial form, feel the need to strictly control the movement of this nomad science (it entrusted the Templars with the responsibility of determining its locations and objects, governing the work sites, and regulating construction), but the secular State, in its royal form, turned against the Templars themselves, banning the guilds for a number of reasons, at least one of which was the prohibition of this operative or minor geometry.

Is Anne Querrien right to find yet another echo of the

same story in the case of bridges in the eighteenth century? Doubtless, the conditions were very different, for the division of labor according to State norms was by then an accomplished fact. But the fact remains that in the government agency in charge of bridges and road-ways, roadways were under a well-centralized adminis-tration while bridges were still the object of active, dynamic and collective experimentation. Trudaine or-ganized unusual, open "general assemblies" in his home. Perronet took as his inspiration a supple model originat-ing in the Orient: the bridge should not choke or obstruct the river. To the heaviness of the bridge, to the striated space of thick and regular piles, he opposed the thinning and discontinuity of the piles, surbasement and vault, the lightness and continuous variation of the whole. But his attempt soon ran up against principled opposition; the State, in naming Perronet director of the school, followed a frequently used procedure that inhibited experimenta-tion more than crowning its achievements. The whole history of the Ecole des Ponts et Chaussées (School of Bridges and Roadways) illustrates how this old, plebeian "corps" was subordinated to the Ecole des Mines, the Ecole des Travaux Publics, and the Ecole Polytechnique, at the same time as its activities were increasingly nor-malized.[27] We thus come to the question, what is a collective *body (corps)*? Undoubtedly, the great collective bodies of a State are differentiated and hierarchical organisms that on the one hand enjoy a monopoly over a power or function, and on the other hand send out local representatives. They have a special relation to families, because they interlink the family model and the State model, and regard themselves as "great families" of functionaries, clerks, intendants or farmers. Yet it seems that in many of these collective bodies there is something else at work that does not fit into this schema. It is not just their obstinate defense of their privileges. It is also their aptitude—even caricatural or seriously deformed—to constitute themselves as a war machine, following other models, another dynamism, a nomadic ambition, over against the State. As an example, there is the very old problem of the *lobby,* a group with fluid contours, whose position is very ambiguous in relation to the State it wishes to "influence" and the war machine it wishes to promote, to whatever ends.[28]

A *body (corps)* is not reducible to an *organism,* any more than *esprit de corps* is reducible to the soul of an organism. Spirit is not better, but it is volatile, whereas the soul is weighted, a center of gravity. Must we invoke a military origin of the collective body and *esprit de corps*? "Military" is not the part that counts, but rather the distant nomadic origin. Ibn Khaldün defines the nomad war machine by: families or lineages PLUS *esprit de corps.* The war machine entertains a relation to families that is very different from its relation to the State. The family, rather than a fundamental cell, is for the war machine a band vector, such that a genealogy is transferred from one family to another according to the aptitude of a given family at a given time to realize the maximum of "agnatic solidarity." Here, it is not the public eminence of a family that determines its place in a State organism, but the reverse, it is the secret potential *(puissance)* or potency *(vertu)* for solidarity, and the corresponding genealogical mobility, which determine its eminence in a war body.[29] This has to do neither with the monopoly of an organic power *(pouvoir)* nor with local representation, but is related to the potential *(puis-*

sance) of a vortical body in a nomad space. Of course, the
great bodies of a modern State can hardly be thought of
as Arab tribes. What we wish to say, rather, is that
collective bodies always have fringes or minorities that
reconstitute equivalents of the war machine—in sometimes quite unforseen forms—in specific assemblages
such as building bridges or cathedrals, or rendering
judgments, or making music, or instituting a science, a
technology . . . A collective body of captains asserts its
demands through the organization of the officers and the
organism of the superior officers. There are always
periods when the State as organism has problems with its
own collective bodies, when these bodies, claiming certain privileges, are forced in spite of themselves to open
onto something that surpasses them, a short revolutionary instant, an experimental surge. A confused situation; each time it occurs, it is necessary to analyze
tendencies and poles, the nature of the movements. All of
a sudden, it is as if the collective body of the notary
publics were advancing like Arabs or Indians, then
regrouping and reorganizing: a comic opera where you
never know what is going to happen next (even the cry,
"The police are with us!," is sometimes heard).

Husserl speaks of a protogeometry that addresses
vague, in other words vagabond or nomadic, morpho-
logical essences. These essences are distinct from sensible
things, but also from ideal, royal or imperial essences.
Protogeometry, the science dealing with them, is itself
vague, in the etymological sense of "vagabond": it is
neither inexact like sensible things, nor exact like ideal
essences, but *anexact, yet rigorous* ("essentially and not
accidently inexact"). The circle is an organic, ideal, fixed
essence, but roundness is a vague and fluent essence,

distinct both from the circle and things that are round (a vase, a wheel, the sun . . .). A theorematic figure is a fixed essence, but its transformations, distortions, ablations and augmentations, all of its variations, form problematic figures that are vague yet rigorous, "lens-shaped," "umbelliform," or "indented." It could be said that vague essences extract from things a determination which is more than thinghood *(choséité)*, which is that of *corporeality (corporéité)*, and which perhaps even implies an *esprit de corps*.[30] But why does Husserl see this as a protogeometry, a kind of half-way point and not a pure science? Why does he make pure essences dependent upon a passage to the limit, when any passage to the limit belongs as such to the vague? What we have, rather, are two formally different conceptions of science, and, ontologically, a single field of interaction in which royal science is perpetually appropriating the contents of vague or nomad science, and nomad science is perpetually releasing the contents of royal science. At the limit, all that counts is the constantly moving borderline.

In Husserl (and also in Kant, though in the opposite direction: roundness as the "schema" of the circle), we find a very accurate appreciation of the irreducibility of nomad science, but simultaneously the concern of a man of the State, or one who sides with the State, to maintain a legislative and constituent primacy for royal science. Whenever this primacy is taken for granted, nomad science is made out to be a prescientific, or parascientific, or subscientific agency. And most importantly, it is no longer possible to understand the relations between science and technology, between science and practice, because nomad science is not a simple technology or practice, but a scientific field in which the problem of these relations is brought out and resolved in an entirely different way than from the point of view of royal science.

The State is perpetually producing and reproducing ideal circles, but a war machine is necessary to make something round. Thus the specific characteristics of nomad science are what need to be determined in order to understand both the repression it encounters and the interaction "containing" it.

Nomad science does not entertain the same relation to work as royal science. Not that the division of labor in nomad science is any less thorough; it is different. We know about the problems States have always had with journeymen's associations, or *compagnonnages*, the nomadic or itinerant bodies of the type formed by masons, carpenters, smiths, etc. Settling, sedentarizing labor-power, regulating the movement of the flow of labor, assigning it channels and conduits, forming corporations in the sense of organisms, and, for the rest, relying on forced manpower recruited on the spot (corvée) or among indigents (charity workshops)—this has always been one of the principal affairs of the State, which undertook to conquer both a *band vagabondage* and a *body nomadism*. Let us return to the example of Gothic architecture for a reminder of how extensively the journeymen traveled, building cathedrals near and far, scattering construction sites across the land, drawing on an active and passive power *(puissance)* (mobility and the strike) that was far from convenient for the State. The State's response was to take over management of the construction sites, merging all the divisions of labor together in the supreme distinction between the intellectual and the manual, the theoretical and the practical, fashioned after the difference between "governors" and "governed." In the nomad sciences, as in the royal sciences, we find the existence of a "plane," but not at all in the same way. The ground-level plane of the Gothic journeyman stands in contrast to the metric plane of the architect, which is on paper and offsite. The plane of consistency or composition stands in contrast to another plane, that of organization or formation. Stone-cutting by squaring stands in contrast to stone-cutting using templates, which implies the erection of a model for reproduction. Not only can it be said that there is no a longer a need for skilled, or qualified, labor, but that there is a need for unskilled, or unqualified, labor, for a dequalification of labor. The State does not give power *(pouvoir)* to the intellectuals or conceptual innovators; on the contrary, it makes them a strictly dependent organ with an autonomy that is only imagined, yet is sufficient to divest those whose job it becomes simply to reproduce or implement of all of their power *(puissance)*. This does not shield the State from more trouble, this time with the body of intellectuals it itself engendered, but which asserts new nomadic and political claims.

In any case, if the State is always finding it necessary to repress the nomad and minor sciences, if it opposes vague essences and the operative geometry of the trait, it does so not because the content of these sciences is inexact or imperfect, or because of their magic or initiatory character, but because they imply a division of labor opposed to the norms of the State. The difference is not extrinsic: the way in which a science, or a conception of science, participates in the organization of the social field, and in particular induces a division of labor, is part of that science itself. Royal science is inseparable from a "hylomorphic" model implying both a form that organizes matter, and a matter prepared for the form; it has often been shown that this schema derives less from technology or life than from a society divided into governors and governed, and later, intellectuals and manual laborers. What characterizes it is that all matter is assigned to content, while all form passes into expression. It seems that nomad science is more immediately sensitive to the connection between content and expression in themselves, each of these two terms encompassing both form and matter. Thus matter, in nomad science, is never prepared and therefore homogenized matter, but is essentially laden with singularities (which constitute a form of content). And neither is expression formal; it is inseparable from pertinent traits (which constitute a matter of expression). This is an entirely different schema, as we shall see. We can get a preliminary idea of this situation by recalling the most general characteristic of nomad art, in which a dynamic connection between support and ornament replaces the matter-form dialectic. From the point of view of nomad science, which presents itself as an art as much as a technique, the division of labor fully exists, but does not employ the form-matter duality (even in the case of one-to-one correspondences). Rather, it *follows* the connections between singularities of matter and traits of expression, and lodges on the level of these connections, whether they be natural or forced.[31] This is another organization of work and of the social field through work.

It is instructive to contrast two models of science, after the manner of Plato in the *Timaeus*.[32] One could be called *Compars*, and the other *Dispars*. The compars is the legal or legalist model employed by royal science. The search for laws consists in extracting constants, even if those constants are only relations between variables (equations). An invariable form for variables, a variable matter of the invariant: such is the foundation of the hylomorphic schema. But for the *dispars* as an element of nomad science the relevant distinction is material-forces rather than matter-form. Here, it is not exactly a question of extracting constants from variables, but of placing the variables themselves in a state of continuous variation. If there are still equations, they are adequations, inequations, differential equations irreducible to the algebraic form and inseparable from a sensible intuition of variation. They seize or determine singularities in the matter, instead of constituting a general form. They effect individuations by way of events or haecceities, not by way of the "object" as a compound of matter and form; vague essences are nothing other than haecceities.

In all these respects, there is an opposition between the *logos* and the *nomos*, the law and the *nomos*, prompting the comment that the law still "savors of morality."[33] This does not mean, however, that the legal model knows nothing of forces, the play of forces. That it does can be easily seen in the homogeneous space corresponding to the *compars*. Homogeneous space is in no way a smooth space; on the contrary, it is the form of striated space. The space of *pillars*. It is striated by the fall of bodies, the verticals of gravity, the distribution of matter into parallel layers, the lamellar and laminar movement of flows. These parallel verticals have formed an independent dimension capable of spreading everywhere, of formalizing all the other dimensions, of striating all of space in all of its directions, so as to render it homogeneous. The vertical distance between two points provided the mode of comparison for the horizontal distance between two other points. Universal attraction became the law of all laws, in that it set the rule for the one-to-one correspondence between two bodies; and each time science discovered a new field, it sought to formalize it in the same mode as the field of gravity. Even chemistry became a royal science only by virtue of an entire theoretical elaboration of the notion of weight. Euclidean space is founded on the famous parallel postulate, but the parallels in question are in the first place gravitational parallels, and correspond to the forces exerted by gravity on all the elements of a body presumed to fill that space. It is the point of application of the resultant of all of these parallel forces that remains invariable when their common direction is changed or the body is rotated (the *center of gravity*). In short, it seems that the force of gravity lies at the basis of a laminar, striated, homogeneous and centered space; it forms the foundation for those multiplicities termed metric, or arborescent, the dimensions of which are independent of the situation and are expressed with the aid of units and points (movements from one point to another). It was not some metaphysical concern, but an effectively scientific one, that frequently led scientists in the nineteenth century to ask if all forces were not reducible to gravity, or rather to the form of attraction that gives gravity a universal value (a constant relation for all variables) and biunique import (two bodies at a time, and no more . . .). It is the form of interiority of all science.

The *nomos*, or the dispars, is entirely different. Not that the other forces refute gravity or contradict attraction. Though it is true that they do not go against them, they do not result from them either, they do not depend on them, but bear witness to events that are always supplementary or of "variable affects." Each time a new *field* opened up in science—under conditions making this a far more important notion than that of form or object—it proved to be irreducible to the field of attraction and the model of the gravitational forces, although not contradicting them. It affirmed a "more" or an excess, and lodged itself in that excess, that deviation. When chemistry took a decisive step forward, it was always by adding to the force of weight liaisons of another type (for example electric) that transformed the nature of chemical equations.[34] But it will be noted that the simplest considerations of velocity immediately introduce the difference between vertical descent and curvilinear motion, or more generally between the straight line and the curve, in the differential form of the clinamen, or the smallest deviation, the minimum excess. Smooth space is precisely the space of the smallest deviation: therefore it has no homogeneity, except between infinitely proximate points, and the linking of proximities is effected independently of any determined path. It is a space of contact, of small tactile or manual actions of contact, rather than a visual space like Euclid's striated space. Smooth space is a field without conduits or channels. A field, a heterogeneous smooth space, is wedded to a very particular type of multiplicity: nonmetric, acentered, rhizomatic multiplicities which occupy space without "counting" it and can "only be explored by legwork." They do not meet the visual condition of being observable from a point in space external to them; examples are the system of sounds, or even of colors, in opposition to Euclidean space.

When we oppose speed and slowness, the quick and

the weighty, *Celeritas and Gravitas*, this must not be seen
as a quantitative opposition, nor as a mythological
structure (although Dumézil has established the mythological importance of this opposition, precisely in relation to the State apparatus and its natural "gravity"). The
opposition is both qualitative and scientific, to the extent
that speed is not only an abstract characteristic of
movement in general, but is incarnated in a moving body
that deviates, however slightly, from its line of descent or
gravity. *Slow and rapid are not quantitative degrees of
movement, but two types of qualified movement,* whatever the speed of the former or the tardiness of the latter.
Strictly speaking, it cannot be said that a body that is
dropped has a speed, however fast it falls, but rather that
it has an infinitely decreasing slowness in accordance
with the law of falling bodies. Laminar movement which
striates space, which goes from one point to another, is
weighty; but rapidity, celerity, only apply to movement
which deviates to the minimum extent and thereafter
assumes a vortical motion, occupying a smooth space,
actually tracing smooth space itself. In this space, matter-
flow can no longer be cut into parallel layers, and
movement no longer allows itself to be hemmed into
biunique relations between points. In this sense, the role
of the qualitative opposition gravity-celerity, heavy-light,
slow-rapid is not that of a quantifiable scientific determination, but of a condition that is coextensive to science,
and that regulates both the separation and the mixing of
the two models, their possible interpenetration, the domination of one by the other, their alternative. And the best
formulation, that of Michel Serres, is indeed couched in
terms of an alternative, whatever mixes or compositions
there may be: "Physics is reducible to two sciences, a

general theory of routes and paths, and a global theory of waves."[35]

A distinction must be made between two types of science, or scientific procedures: one consists in "reproducing," the other in "following." The first has to do with reproduction, iteration and reiteration; the other, having to do with itineration, is the sum of the itinerant, ambulant sciences. Itineration is too readily reduced to a modality of technology , or of the application and verification of science. But this is not the case: *following is not at all the same thing as reproducing,* and one never follows in order to reproduce. The ideal of reproduction, deduction or induction is part of royal science, at all times and in all places, and treats differences of time and place as so many variables, the constant form of which is extracted precisely by the law: for the same phenomena to recur in a gravitational and striated space it is sufficient for the same conditions to obtain, or for the same constant relation to hold between the differing conditions and the variable phenomena. Reproducing implies the permanence of a fixed point of *view* that is external to what is reproduced: watching the flow from the bank. But following is something different from the ideal of reproduction. Not better, just different. One is obliged to follow when one is in search of the "singularities" of a matter, or rather of a material, and not out to discover a form; when one escapes the force of gravity to enter a field of celerity; when one ceases to contemplate the course of a laminar flow in a determinate direction, to be carried away by a vortical flow; when one is involved with the continuous variation of variables, instead of extracting constants from them, etc. And the meaning of Earth completely changes: with the legal model, one is constantly reterritorializing around a point of view, on a domain, according to a set of constant relations; but with the ambulant model, the process of deterritorialization constitutes and extends the territory itself. "Go first to your old plant and watch carefully the watercourse made by the rain. By now the rain must have carried the seeds far away. Watch the crevices made by the runoff, and from them determine the direction of the flow. Then find the plant that is growing at the farthest point from your plant. All the plants that are growing in between are yours. Later . . . you can extend the size of your territory."[36]

There are itinerant, ambulant sciences that consist in following a flow in a vectorial field across which singularities are scattered like so many "accidents" (problems). For example: why is primitive metallurgy necessarily an ambulant science that confers upon smiths a quasi-nomadic status? It could be objected that in these examples it is still a question of going from one point to another (even if they are singular points) through the intermediary of channels, and that it is still possible to cut the flow into layers. But this is only true to the extent that ambulant procedures and processes are necessarily connected with a striated space—always formalized by royal science—which deprives them of their model, submits them to its own model, and only allows them to exist in the capacity of "technologies" or "applied science." As a general rule, a smooth space, a vectorial field, a nonmetric multiplicity are always translatable, and necessarily translated, into a "compars": a fundamental operation by which one repeatedly overlays upon each point of smooth space a tangent Euclidean space endowed with a sufficient number of dimensions, by which one reintroduces parallelism between two vectors, treating multiplicity as though it were immersed in this homogeneous and striated space of reproduction instead of continuing to follow it in an "exploration by legwork."[37] This is the triumph of the *logos* or the law over the *nomos*. But the complexity of the operation testifies to the existence of resistances that it must overcome. Whenever ambulant procedure and process are returned to their own model, the points regain their position as singularities that exclude all biunique relations, the flow regains its curvilinear and vortical motion that excludes any parallelism between vectors, smooth space reconquers the properties of contact that prevent it from remaining homogeneous and striated. There is always a current preventing the ambulant or itinerant sciences from being completely internalized in the reproductive royal sciences. There is a type of ambulant scientist whom State scientists are forever fighting or integrating or allying with, even going so far as to propose a minor position for them within the legal system of science and technology.

It is not that the ambulant sciences are more saturated with irrational procedures, mystery and magic. They only get that way when they fall into abeyance. And the royal sciences, for their part, also surround themselves with much priestliness and magic. Rather, what comes out in the rivalry between the two models is that the ambulant or nomad sciences do not destine science to take on an autonomous power, or even to have an autonomous development. They do not have the means for that, since they subordinate all their operations to the sensible conditions of intuition and construction— *following* the flow of matter, *tracing and connecting up* smooth space. Everything is situated in an objective zone of fluctuation that is coextensive with reality itself.

However refined or rigorous, "approximate knowledge" is still dependent upon sensitive and sensible evaluations that pose more problems than they solve: problematics is still its only mode. In contrast, what is proper to royal science, to its theorematic or axiomatic power, is to isolate all operations from the conditions of intuition, making them true intrinsic concepts, or "categories." That is precisely why deterritorialization, in this kind of science, implies a reterritorialization in the conceptual apparatus. Without this categorical, apodictic apparatus, the differential operations would be constrained to follow the evolution of a phenomenon; what is more, since the experimentation would be open-air, and the construction at ground level, the coordinates permitting them to be erected as stable models would never become available. Certain of these requirements are translated in terms of "safety": the two cathedrals at Orléans and Beauvais collapsed at the end of the twelfth century, and control calculations are difficult to effect for the constructions of ambulant science. Although safety is a fundamental element in the theoretical norms of the State, and of the political ideal, there is also something else at issue a well. Due to all their procedures (*démarches*), the ambulant sciences quickly overstep the possibility of calculation: they inhabit that "more" that exceeds the space of reproduction, and soon run into problems that are insurmountable from that point of view; they eventually resolve those problems by means of a real-life operation. The solutions are supposed to come from a set of activities which constitute them as non-autonomous. Only royal science, in contrast, has at its disposal a metric power (*puissance*) that can define a conceptual apparatus or an autonomy of science (including the autonomy of experimental science). That is why it is necessary to couple ambulant spaces with a space of homogeneity, without which the laws of physics would depend on particular points in space. But this is less a translation than a constitution: precisely that constitution which the ambulant sciences did not undertake, and do not have the means to undertake. In the field of interaction of the two sciences, the ambulant sciences confine themselves to *inventing problems* the solution of which is linked to an entire set of collective, nonscientific activities, but the *scientific solution* of which depends, on the contrary, on royal science and the way it has transformed the problem by introducing it into its theorematic apparatus and its organization of work. This is somewhat like intuition and intelligence in Bergson, where only intelligence has the scientific means to solve formally the problems posed by intuition, problems that intuition would be content to entrust to the qualitative activities of a humanity engaged in *following* matter . . .[38]

Problem 2: Is there a way to extricate thought from the State model?

Proposition 4: The exteriority of the war machine is attested to, finally, by noology.

Thought contents are sometimes criticized for being too conformist. But the primary question is that of its form. Thought as such is already in conformity with a model that it borrows from the State apparatus, and which defines for it goals and paths, conduits, channels, organs, an entire *organon*. There is thus an image of thought spanning all thought, which is the special object of a "noology," and which is like the State-form developed in thought. And this image has two heads, corresponding to the two poles of sovereignty: the *imperium* of true thinking *(le penser-vrai)* operating by magical capture, seizure or binding, constituting the efficacity of a foundation *(fondation) (mythos)*; a republic of free spirits proceeding by pact or contract, constituting a legislative and juridical organization, carrying the sanction of a ground *(fondement) (logos)*. These two heads are in constant interference in the classical image of thought: a "republic of free spirits whose prince would be the idea of the Supreme Being." And if these two heads are in interference, it is not only because there are many intermediaries and transitions between them, and because the first prepares the way for the second and the second uses and retains the first, but also because, antithetical and complementary, they are necessary to one another. It is not out of the question, however, that in order to pass from one to the other there must occur, "between" them, an event of an entirely different nature, one that hides outside the image, takes place outside.[39] But confining ourselves to the image, it seems that it is not simply a metaphor when we are told of an *imperium* of truth and a republic of spirits. It is the necessary condition for the constitution of thought as principle, or as a form of interiority, as a stratum.

It is easy to see what thought gains from this: a gravity it would never have on its own, a center that makes everything, including the State, appear to exist on its own efficacity or on its own sanction. But the State gains just as much. Indeed, by developing in thought in this way the State-form gains something essential: an entire consensus. Only thought is capable of inventing the fiction of a

State that is universal by right, of elevating the State to the
level of the universality of law. It is as if the sovereign
were left alone in the world, spanned the entire ecumenon, and now dealt only with actual or potential
subjects. It is no longer a question of powerful, extrinsic
organizations, nor of strange bands: the State becomes
the sole principle separating rebel subjects, who are
consigned to the state of nature, from consenting subjects, who rally to its form of their own accord. If it is
advantageous for thought to prop itself up with the State,
it is no less advantageous for the State to extend itself in
thought, and to be sanctioned by it as the unique,
universal form. The particularity of States becomes merely an accident of fact; as is their possible perversity, or
their imperfection. For the modern State defines itself in
principle as "the rational and reasonable organization of
a community": the only remaining particularity a community has is interior or moral (*the spirit of a people*), at
the same time as the community is funneled by its
organization toward the harmony of a universal (*absolute spirit*). The State gives thought a form of interiority,
and thought gives that interiority a form of universality:
"the goal of worldwide organization is the satisfaction of
reasonable individuals within particular free States." The
exchange that takes place between the State and reason is
a curious one; but that exchange is also an analytic
proposition, since realized reason is identified with the
State of right, just as the State in fact is the becoming of
reason.[40] In so-called modern philosophy, and in the
so-called modern or rational State, everything revolves
around the legislator and the subject. The State must
realize the distinction between the legislator and the
subject under formal conditions permitting thought, for

its part, to conceptualize their identity. Be obedient always. The better you obey, the more you will be master, for you will only be obeying pure reason, in other words yourself . . .

Ever since philosophy assigned itself the role of ground it has been giving the established powers its blessing, and tracing *(décalquer)* its doctrine of faculties onto the organs of State power. Common sense, the unity of all the faculties at the center constituted by the Cogito, is the State consensus raised to the absolute. This was most notably the great operation of the Kantian "critique," renewed and developed by Hegelianism. Kant was constantly criticizing bad usages, the better to consecrate the function. It is not at all surprising that the philosopher has become a public professor or State functionary. It was all over the moment the State-form inspired an image of thought. With full reciprocity. Doubtless, the image itself assumes different contours in accordance with the variations on this form: it has not always delineated or designated the philosopher, and will not always delineate him. It is possible to pass from a magical function to a rational function. The poet in the archaic imperial State was able to play the role of image trainer.[41] In modern States, the sociologist succeeded in replacing the philosopher (as for example when Durkheim and his disciples set out to give the republic a secular model of thought). Even today, psychoanalysis lays claim to the role of *Cogitatio universalis* as the thought of the Law, in a magical return. And there are quite a few other competitors and pretenders. Noology, which is distinct from ideology, is precisely the study of images of thought, and their historicity. In a sense, it could be said that all this has no importance, that thought has never had anything but laughable gravity. But that is all it requires: for us not to take it seriously. Because that makes it all the easier for it to think for us, and to be forever engendering new functionaries. Because the less people take thought seriously, the more they think in conformity with what the State wants. Truly, what man of the State has not dreamed of that paltry impossible thing—to be a thinker?

But noology is confronted by counterthoughts, which are violent in their acts, discontinuous in their appearances, and the existence of which is mobile in history. These are the acts of a "private thinker," as opposed to the public professor: Kierkegaard, Nietzsche, or even Chestov . . . Wherever they dwell, it is the steppe or the desert. They destroy images. Nietzsche's *Schopenhauer as Educator* is perhaps the greatest critique ever directed against the image of thought and its relation to the State. "Private thinker," however, is not a satisfactory expression, because it exaggerates interiority, when it is a question of *outside thought*.[42] To place thought in an immediate relation with the outside, with the forces of the outside, in short to make thought a war machine, is a strange undertaking, the precise procedures of which can be studied in Nietzsche (the aphorism, for example, is very different from the maxim, for a maxim, in the republic of letters, is like an organic State act or sovereign judgment, whereas an aphorism always awaits its meaning from a new external force, a final force that must conquer or subjugate it, utilize it). There is another reason why "private thinker" is not a good expression: although it is true that this counterthought attests to an absolute solitude, it is an extremely populous solitude, like the desert itself, a solitude already interlaced with a people to come, one that invokes and awaits that people, existing only through it, though it is not yet here . . . "We are lacking that final force, in the absence of a people to bear us. We are looking for that popular support . . ."

Every thought is already a tribe, the opposite of a State. And this form of exteriority of thought is not at all symmetrical to the form of interiority. Strictly speaking, symmetry only exists between different poles or focal points *(foyers)* of interiority. But the form of exteriority of thought—the force that is always external to itself, or the final force, the nth power—is not at all *another image* in opposition to the image inspired by the State apparatus. It is, rather, a force that destroys both the image *and* its copies, the model *and* its reproductions, every possibility of subordinating thought to a model of the True, the Just or the Right (Cartesian truth, the Kantian just, Hegelian right, etc.). A "method" is the striated space of the *cogitatio universalis,* and traces a path that must be followed from one point to another. But the form of exteriority situates thought in a smooth space that it must occupy without counting, and for which there is no possible method, no conceivable reproduction, but only relays, intermezzos, resurgences. Thought is like the Vampire, it has no image, either to constitute a model of or to copy. In the smooth space of Zen, the arrow does not go from one point to another, but is taken up at any point, to be sent to any other point, and tends to permute with the archer and the target. The problem of the war machine is that of relaying, even with modest means, not that of the architectonic model or the monument. An ambulant people of relayers, rather than a model society. "Nature propels the philosopher into mankind like an arrow; it takes no aim but hopes the arrow will stick somewhere. But countless times it misses and is depressed at the fact. . . . The artist and the philosopher are evidence against the purposiveness of nature as regards the means it employs, though they are also first-rate evidence as to the wisdom of its purpose. They strike home at only a few, while they ought to strike home at everybody—and even these few are not struck with the force with which the philosopher and artist launch their shot.''[43]

We have in mind in particular two pathetic texts, in the sense that in them thought is truly a *pathos* (an *antilogos* and an *antimythos*). One is a text by Artaud, in his letters to Jacques Rivière, explaining that thought operates on the basis of a *central breakdown,* that it lives solely by its own incapacity to take on form, bringing into relief only traits of expression in a material, developing peripherally, in a pure milieu of exteriority, as a function of singularities impossible to universalize, of circumstances impossible to interiorize. The other is the text of Kleist, "On the Gradual Formation of Ideas in Speech" *("Über die allmächliche Verfertigung der Gedanken beim Reden"):* Kleist denounces the central interiority of the concept as a means of control—the control of speech, of language, but also of affects, circumstances and even chance. He distinguishes this from thought as a proceeding *(procès)* and a process *(processus),* a bizarre anti-Platonic dialogue, an anti-dialogue between brother and sister where one speaks before knowing while the other relays before having understood: this, Kleist says, is the thought of the *Gemüt,* which proceeds like a general in a war machine should, or like a body charged with electricity, with pure intensity. "I mix inarticulate sounds, lengthen transitional terms, as well as using appositions when they are unnecessary." Gain some time, and then perhaps renounce, or wait. The necessity of not having control over language, of being a foreigner in one's own language, in order to draw speech to oneself and "bring something incomprehensible into the world." Such is the form of exteriority, the relation between brother and sister, the becoming-woman of the thinker, the becoming-thought of the woman: the *Gemüt* that refuses to be controlled, that forms a war machine. A thought grappling with exterior forces instead of being gathered up in an interior form, operating by relays instead of forming an image; an event-thought, a haecceity, instead of a subject-thought, a problem-thought instead of an essence-thought or theorem; a thought that appeals to a people instead of taking itself for a government ministry. Is it by chance that whenever a "thinker" shoots an arrow, there is a man of the State, a shadow or an image of a man of the State, that counsels and admonishes him, and wants to assign him a target or "aim"? Jacques Rivière does not hesitate to respond to Artaud: work at it, keep on working, things will come out alright, you will succeed in finding a method and in learning to express clearly what you think in essence *(Cogitatio universalis)*. Rivière is not a head of State, but he would not be the last in the Nouvelle Revue Française to mistake himself for the secret prince in a republic of letters or the gray eminence in a State of right. Lenz and Kleist confronted Goethe, that grandiose genius, of all men of letters a veritable man of the State. But that is not the worst of it: the worst is the way the texts of Kleist and Artaud themselves have ended up becoming monuments, inspiring a model to be copied—one far more insidious than the others—for the artificial stammerings and innumerable tracings *(décalques)* which claim to be their equal.

The classical image of thought, and the striating of

mental space it effects, aspires to universality. It in effect operates with two "universals," the Whole as the final ground of being or all-encompassing horizon, and the Subject as the principle that converts being into being-for-us.[44] *Imperium* and republic. Between the two, all of the varieties of the real and the true find their place in a striated mental space, from the double point of view of Being and the Subject, under the direction of a "universal method." It is now easy for us to characterize the nomad thought that rejects this image, and proceeds otherwise. It does not ally itself with a universal thinking subject, but on the contrary with a singular race; and it does not ground itself in an all-encompassing totality, but is on the contrary deployed in a horizonless milieu that is a smooth space, steppe, desert or sea. An entirely different type of adequation is established here, between the race defined as "tribe" and smooth space defined as "milieu." A tribe in the desert instead of a universal subject within the horizon of all-encompassing Being. Kenneth White recently stressed this dissymmetrical complementarity between a tribe-race (the Celts, those who feel they are Celts) and a space-milieu (the Orient, the Gobi Desert . . .): White demonstrates that this strange composite, the marriage of the Celt and the Orient, inspires a properly nomad thought that sweeps up English literature and constitutes American literature.[45] Immediately, we clearly see the dangers, the profound ambiguities that inhere in this enterprise, as if each effort and each creation faced a possible infamy. For what can be done to prevent the theme of a race from turning into a racism, a dominant and all-encompassing fascism, or into a sect and a folklore, micro-fascisms? And what can be done to prevent the Oriental pole from becoming a phantasy that reactivates all the fascisms in a different way, and also all the folklores, yoga, Zen, and karate? It is certainly not enough to travel to escape phantasy; and it is certainly not by invoking a past, real or mythical, that one avoids racism. But here again, the criteria for making the distinction are simple, whatever the de facto mixes that obscure them at a given level, at a given moment. The tribe-race exists only at the level of an oppressed race, and in the name of the oppression it suffers: there is no race but inferior, minoritarian, there is no dominant race, a race is not defined by its purity but rather by the impurity conferred upon it by a system of domination. Bastard and mixed-blood are the true names of race. Rimbaud said it all on this point: only he can invoke race who says, "I have always been of an inferior race . . . ./ I am of an inferior race for all eternity . . . ./ There I am on the Breton shore . . . ./ I am a beast, a nigger . . . ./ I am of a distant race: my ancestors were Norsemen."[46] In the same way that race is not something to be rediscovered, the Orient is not something to be imitated: it only exists in the construction of a smooth space, just as race only exists in the constitution of a tribe that peoples and traverses a smooth space. All of thought is a becoming, a double becoming, rather than the attribute of a Subject and the representation of a Whole.

Axiom 2: The war machine is the invention of the nomads (insofar as it is exterior to the State apparatus and distinct from the military institution). As such, the war machine has three aspects, a spatio-geographic aspect, an arithmetic or algebraic aspect, and an affective aspect.

Proposition 5: Nomad existence necessarily effec-
tuates the conditions of the war machine in space.

The nomad has a territory, he follows customary
paths, he goes from one point to another, he is not
ignorant of points (water points, dwelling points, assembly points, etc.). But the question is what in nomad life is
a principle and what is only a consequence. To begin
with, although the points determine paths, they are
strictly subordinated to the paths they determine, the
reverse of what happens with the sedentary. The water
point is reached only in order to be left behind, every
point is a relay and exists only as a relay. A path is always
between two points, but the in-between has taken on all
the consistency, and enjoys both an autonomy and a
direction of its own. The life of the nomad is the
intermezzo. Even the elements of his dwelling are conceived in terms of the trajectory that is forever mobilizing
them.[47] The nomad is not at all the same as the migrant;
for the migrant goes principally from one point to
another, even if the second point is uncertain, unforseen
or not well localized. But the nomad only goes from point
to point as a consequence and as a factual necessity: in
principle, points for him are relays along a trajectory.
Nomads and migrants can mix in many ways, or form a
common aggregate; their causes and conditions are no
less distinct for that (for example, those who joined
Mohammed at Medina had a choice between a nomadic
or bedouin pledge, and pledge of hegira or emigration).[48]
    Secondly, even though the nomadic trajectory may
follow trails or customary routes, it does not fulfill
the function of the sedentary road, which is to *par-*
cel out a closed space to people, assigning each

person a share and regulating the communication between shares. The nomadic trajectory does the opposite,
it *distributes people (or animals) in an open space,* one
that is indefinite and noncommunicating. The *nomos*
came to designate the law, but that was originally
because it was distribution, a mode of distribution. It is a
very special kind of distribution, one without division
into shares, in a space without borders or enclosure. The
nomos is the consistency of a fuzzy aggregate: it is in this
sense that it stands in opposition to the law or the *polis,* as
the backcountry, a mountainside or the vague expanse
around a city ("either nomos or polis"[49]). There is
therefore, and this is the third point, a significant difference between the spaces: sedentary space is striated, by
walls, enclosures and roads between enclosures, while
nomad space is smooth, marked only by "traits" that are
effaced and displaced with the trajectory. Even the
lamella of the desert slide over each other, producing an
inimitable sound. The nomad distributes himself in a
smooth space, he occupies, inhabits, holds that space;
that is his territorial principle. It is therefore false to
define the nomad by movement. Toynbee is profoundly
right to suggest that the nomad is on the contrary *he who
does not move.* Whereas the migrant leaves behind a
milieu that has become amorphous or hostile, the nomad
is one who does not depart, does not want to depart, who
clings to the smooth space left by the receding forest,
where the steppe or the desert advance, and who invents
nomadism as a response to this challenge.[50] Of course,
the nomad moves, but while seated, and he is only seated
while moving (the Bedouin galloping, knees on the
saddle, sitting on the soles of his upturned feet, "a feat of
balance"). The nomad knows how to wait, he has infinite

patience. Immobility and speed, catatonia and rush, a "stationary process," station as process—these traits of Kleist's are eminently those of the nomad. It is thus necessary to make a distinction between *speed* and *movement*: a movement may be very fast, but that does not give it speed; a speed may be very slow, or even immobile, yet it is still speed. Movement is extensive, speed is intensive. Movement designates the relative character of a body considered as "one," and which goes from point to point; *speed, on the contrary, constitutes the absolute character of a body whose irreducible parts (atoms) occupy or fill a smooth space in the manner of a vortex,* with the possibility of springing up at any point. (It is therefore not surprising that reference has been made to spiritual voyages effected without relative movement, but in intensity, in one place: these are part of nomadism). In short, we will say by convention that only the nomad has absolute movement, in other words speed; vortical or swirling movement is an essential feature of his war machine.

It is in this sense that the nomad has no points, paths or land, even though he does by all appearances. If the nomad can be called the Deterritorialized *par excellence*, it is precisely because there is no reterritorialization *afterwards* as with the migrant, or upon *something else* as with the sedentary (the sedentary's relation with the earth is mediatized by something else, a property regime, a State apparatus . . .). With the nomad, on the contrary, it is deterritorialization that constitutes the relation to the earth, to such a degree that the nomad reterritorializes on deterritorialization itself. It is the earth that deterritorializes itself, in a way that provides the nomad with a territory. The land ceases to be land, tending to become

simply ground *(sol)* or support. The earth does not
become deterritorialized in its global and relative movement, but at specific locations, at the spot where the
forest recedes, or where the steppe and the desert advance. Hubac is right to say that nomadism is explainable
less by universal changes in climate (which relate instead
to migrations) as by the "divagation of local climates."[51]
The nomad is there, on the land, wherever there forms a
smooth space that gnaws, and tends to grow, in all
directions. The nomad inhabits these places, he remains
in them, and he himself makes them grow, for it has been
established that the nomad makes the desert no less than
he is made by it. He is a vector of deterritorialization. He
adds desert to desert, steppe to steppe, by a series of local
operations the orientation and direction of which end-
lessly vary.[52] The sand desert does not only have oases,
which are like fixed points, but also rhizomatic vegeta-
tion that is temporary and shifts location according to
local rains, bringing changes in the direction of the
crossings.[53] The same terms are used to describe ice
deserts as sand deserts: there is no line separating earth
and sky; there is no intermediate distance, no perspective
or contour, visibility is limited; and yet there is an
extraordinarily fine topology that does not rely on points
or objects, but on haecceities, on sets of relations (winds,
undulations of snow or sand, the song of the sand or the
creaking of ice, the tactile qualities of both); it is a tactile
space, or rather "haptic," a sonorous much more than a
visual space . . .[54] The variability, the polyvocity of
directions, is an essential feature of smooth spaces of the
rhizome type, and it alters their cartography.

The nomad, nomad space, is localized and not delimited. What is both limited and limiting is striated

space, the *relative global*: it is limited in its parts, which are assigned constant directions, are oriented in relation to one another, divisible by boundaries, and can be fit together; what is limiting (*limes* or wall, and no longer boundary), is this composite in relation to the smooth spaces it "contains," the growth of which it slows or prevents, and which it restricts or places outside. Even when the nomad sustains its effects, he does not belong to this relative global, where one passes from one point to another, from one region to another. Rather, he is in a *local absolute*, an absolute that is manifested locally, and engendered in a series of local operations of varying orientations: desert, steppe, ice, sea.

Making the absolute appear in a particular place—is that not a very general characteristic of religion (recognizing that the nature of the appearance, and the legitimacy, or lack thereof, of the images which reproduce it are open to debate)? But the sacred place of religion is fundamentally a center which repels the obscure *nomos*. The absolute of religion is essentially a horizon that encompasses, and, if the absolute itself appears at a particular place, it does so in order to establish a solid and stable center for the global. The encompassing role of smooth spaces (desert, steppe or ocean) in monotheism has been frequently noted. In short, religion converts the absolute. Religion is in this sense a piece in the State apparatus (in both of its forms, the "bond" and the "pact or alliance"), even if it has within itself the power *(puissance)* to elevate this model to the level of the universal or to constitute an absolute *Imperium*. But for the nomad the terms of the question are totally different: locality is not delimited; the absolute, then, does not appear at a particular place, but becomes a nonlimited locality; the coupling of the place and the absolute is not achieved in a centered, oriented globalization or universalization, but in an infinite succession of local operations. Limiting ourselves to this opposition between points of view, it may be observed that nomads do not provide a favorable terrain for religion; the man of war is always committing an offense against the priest or the god. The nomads have a vague, literally vagabond "monotheism," and content themselves with that, and with their ambulant fires. There is among the nomads a sense of the absolute, but a singularly atheistic one. The universalist religions that have had dealings with nomads—Moses, Mohammed, even Christianity with the Nestorian heresy— have always encountered problems in this regard, and have run up against what they have termed obstinate impiety. These religions are not, in effect, separable from a firm and constant orientation, from an imperial State of right, even, and especially, in the absence of a State in fact; they have promoted an ideal of sedentarization, and addressed themselves more to the migrant components than the nomadic ones. Even early Islam favored the theme of the hegira, or migration, over nomadism; rather, it was by way of certain schisms (such as the Khârijî movement) that it won over the Arab or Berber nomads.[55]

However, it is not an exhaustive approach to establish a simple opposition between two points of view, religion-nomadism. For monotheistic religion, at the deepest level of its tendency to project a universal or spiritual State over the entire ecumenon, is not without ambivalence or fringe areas; it goes beyond even the ideal limits of the State, even the imperial State, entering a more indistinct zone, an outside of States where it has the possibility of undergoing a singular mutation or adaptation. We are referring to religion as an element in a war machine, and the idea of holy war as the motor of that machine. The *prophet*, as opposed to the state personality of the king and the religious personality of the priest, traces the movement by which a religion becomes a war machine or passes over to the side of such a machine. It has often been said that Islam, and the prophet Mohammed, performed such a conversion of religion, and constituted a veritable *esprit de corps*: in the formula of Georges Bataille, "early Islam, a society reduced to the military enterprise." This is what the West invokes in order to justify its antipathy toward Islam. Yet the Crusades were a properly Christian adventure of this type. The prophets may very well condemn nomad life; the war machine may very well favor the movement of migration and the ideal of establishment; religion in general may very well compensate for its specific deterritorialization with a spiritual and even physical reterritorialization, which in the case of the holy war assumes the well-directed character of a conquest of the holy lands as the center of the world—but despite all of that, when religion sets itself up a war machine, it mobilizes and liberates a formidable charge of nomadism or absolute deterritorialization, it doubles the migrant with an accompanying nomad, or with the potential nomad the migrant is in the process of becoming, and finally, it turns its dream of an absolute State back against the State-form[56] And this turning against is no less a part of the "essence" of religion than that dream. The history of the Crusades is marked by the most astonishing series of directional changes: the firm orientation toward the holy lands as a center to reach often seems nothing more than a pretext. But it would be wrong to say that the play of self-interest, or economic, commercial or political factors, diverted the crusade from its pure path. The idea of the crusade *in itself implies this variability of directions*, broken and changing, and intrinsically possesses all these factors or all these variables from the moment it turns religion into a war machine and simultaneously utilizes and gives rise to the corresponding nomadism.[57] The necessity for maintaining the most rigorous of distinctions between sedentaries, migrants and nomads does not preclude de facto mixes; on the contrary, it makes them in turn all the more necessary. And it is impossible to think of the general process of sedentarization that vanquished the nomads without also envisioning the gusts of local nomadization that carried off sedentaries and doubled migrants (notably, to the benefit of religion).

Smooth or nomad space lies between two striated spaces: that of the forest, with its gravitational verticals, and that of agriculture, with its grids and generalized parallels, its now independent arborescence, its art of extracting the tree and wood from the forest. But being "between" also means that smooth space is controlled by these two flanks, which limit it, oppose its development and assign it as much as possible a communicational role; or on the contrary it means that it turns against them, gnawing away at the forest on one side, on the other side gaining ground on the cultivated lands, affirming a noncommunicating force or a force of *divergence* like a "wedge" digging in. The nomads turn first against the forest and the mountain dwellers, then descend upon the farmers. What we have here is something like the flipside or the outside of the State-form—but in what sense? This form, as a global and relative space, implies a certain

number of components: forest-clearing of fields; agricul-
ture-grid laying; animal raising subordinated to agricultural work and sedentary food production; commerce
based on a constellation of town-country (*polis-nomos*)
communications. When historians inquire into the reasons
for the victory of the West over the Orient, they primarily
mention the following characteristics, which put the
Orient in general at a disadvantage: deforestation rather
than clearing for planting, making it extremely difficult
to extract or even to find wood; cultivation of the type
"rice paddy and garden" rather than arborescence and
field; animal raising for the most part outside the control
of the sedentaries, with the result that they lacked animal
power and meat foods; the low communication content
of the town-country relation, making commerce far less
flexible.[38] the conclusion is not that the State-form is
absent in the Orient. Quite to the contrary, a more rigid
agency becomes necessary in order to retain and reunite
the various components plied by escape vectors.

States always have the same composition; if there is
even one truth in the political philosophy of Hegel, it is
that every State carries within itself the essential moments
of its existence. States are not only made up of people, but
of wood, fields or gardens, animals and commodities.
There is a unity of *composition* of all States, but States
have neither the same *development* nor the same *organization*. In the Orient, the components are much more
disconnected, disjointed, necessitating a great immutable
Form to hold them together: "despotic formations,"
Asian or African, are rocked by incessant revolts, by
secessions and dynastic changes, which nevertheless do
not affect the immutability of the form. In the West, on
the other hand, the interconnectedness of the compo-

nents makes possible transformations of the State-form
through revolution. It is true that the idea of revolution
itself is ambiguous; it is Western insofar as it relates to a
transformation of the State, but Eastern insofar as it
envisions the destruction, the abolition of the State.[59] The
great empires of the Orient, Africa and America run up
against wide-open smooth spaces that penetrate them
and maintain gaps between their components (the *nomos*
does not become countryside, the countryside does not
communicate with the town, large-scale animal raising is
the affair of the nomads, etc.): the Oriental State is in
direct confrontation with a nomad war machine. This
war machine may fall back to the road of integration, and
proceed solely by revolt and dynastic change; nevertheless, it is the war machine, as nomad, that invents the
abolitionist dream and reality. Western States are much
more sheltered in their striated space, and consequently
have much more latitude in holding their components
together; they only confront the nomads indirectly,
through the intermediary of the migrations the nomads
trigger or adopt as their stance.[60]

One of the fundamental tasks of the State is to striate
the space over which it reigns, or to utilize smooth spaces
as a means of communication in the service of striated
space. It is a vital concern of every State not only to
vanquish nomadism, but to control migrations and, more
generally, to establish a zone of rights over an entire
"exterior," over all of the flows traversing the ecumenon.
If it can help it, the State does not dissociate itself from a
process of capture of flows of all kinds, populations,
commodities or commerce, money or capital, etc. There
is still a need for fixed paths in well-defined directions,
which restrict speed, regulate circulation, relativize

movement, and measure in detail the relative movements of subjects and objects. That is why Paul Virilio's thesis is important, when he shows that "the political power of the State is *polis*, police, that is, management of the public ways," and that "the gates of the city, its levies and duties, are barriers, filters against the fluidity of the masses, against the penetration power of migratory packs," people, animals and goods.[61] Gravity, *gravitas*, such is the essence of the State. It is not at all that the State knows nothing of speed; but it requires that movement, even the fastest, cease to be the absolute state of a moving body occupying a smooth space, to become the relative characteristic of a "moved body" going from one point to another in a striated space. In this sense, the State never ceases to decompose, recompose and transform movement, or to regulate speed. The State as town surveyor, converter or highway interchange: the role of the engineer from this point of view.

Speed and absolute movement are not without their laws, but they are the laws of the *nomos*, of the smooth space that deploys it, of the war machine that populates it. If the nomads formed the war machine, it was by inventing absolute speed, by being "synonymous" with speed. And each time there is an operation against the State—subordination, rioting, guerilla warfare or revolution as act—it can be said that a war machine has revived, that a new nomadic potential has appeared, accompanied by the reconstitution of a smooth space or a manner of being in space as though it were smooth (Virilio discusses the importance of the riot or revolutionary theme of "holding the street"). It is in this sense that the response of the State against all that threatens to move beyond it is to striate space. The State does not appropriate the war machine without giving even it the form of relative movement: this was the case with the model of the *fortress* as a regulator of movement, which was precisely the obstacle the nomads came up against, the stumbling block and parry by which absolute vortical movement was broken. Conversely, when a State does not succeed in striating its interior or neighboring space, the flows traversing that State necessarily adopt the stance of a war machine directed against it, deployed in a hostile or rebellious smooth space (even if other States are able to slip their striations in). This was the adventure of China; towards the end of the fourteenth century, and in spite of its very high level of technology in ships and navigation, it turned its back on its huge maritime space, saw its commercial flows turn against it and ally themselves with piracy, and was unable to react except by a politics of immobility, of the massive restriction of commerce, which only reinforces the connection between commerce and the war machine.[62]

The situation is much more complicated than we have led on. The sea is perhaps principal among smooth spaces, the hydraulic model *par excellence*. But the sea is also, of all smooth spaces, the first one attempts were made to striate, to transform into a dependency of the land, with its fixed routes, constant directions, relative movements, a whole counterhydraulic of channels and conduits. One of the reasons for the hegemony of the West was the power *(puissance)* of its State apparatuses to striate the sea by combining the technologies of the North and the Mediterranean and by annexing the Atlantic. But this undertaking had the most unexpected result: the multiplication of relative movements, the intensification of relative speeds in striated space, ended up reconstituting a smooth space or absolute movement. As Virilio emphasizes, the sea became the place of the *fleet in being*, where one no longer goes from one point to another, but rather holds space beginning from any point: instead of striating space, one occupies it with a vector of deterritorialization in perpetual motion. This modern strategy was communicated from the sea to the air, as the new smooth space, but also to the entire Earth considered as desert or sea. As converter and capturer, the State does not just relativize movement, it brings back absolute movement. It does not just go from the smooth to the striated, it reconstitutes smooth space, it brings back the smooth in the wake of the striated. It is true that this new nomadism accompanies a worldwide war machine the organization of which exceeds the State apparatuses, and passes into energy, military-industrial, and multinational complexes. We say this as a reminder that smooth space and the form of exteriority do not have an irresistible revolutionary calling, but change meaning drastically depending on the interactions they are part of and the concrete conditions of their exercise or establishment (for example, the way in which total war and popular war, and even guerilla warfare, borrow one another's methods).[63]

Proposition 6: Nomad existence necessarily implies the numerical elements of a war machine.

Tens, hundreds, thousands, myriads: all armies retain these decimal groupings, to the point that each time they are encountered it is safe to assume the presence of a military organization. Is this not the way an army deterritorializes its soldiers? An army is composed of units, companies and divisions. The Numbers can vary in function, in combination, they can enter into entirely different strategies, but there is always a connection between the Number and the war machine. It is not a question of quantity, but of organization or composition. When the State creates armies, it always applies this principle of numerical organization; but all it does is adopt the principle, at the same time as it appropriates the war machine. For so peculiar an idea—the numerical organization of people—came from to the nomads. It was the Hyksos, conquering nomads, who brought it to Egypt; and when Moses applied it to his people in exodus, it was on the advice of his nomad father-in-law, Jethro the Cinite, and was done is such a way as to constitute a war machine, the elements of which are described in the *Book of Numbers*. The *nomos* is fundamentally numerical, arithmetic. When Greek geometrism is contrasted with Indo-Arab arithmetism, it becomes clear that the latter implies a *nomos* opposable to the logos: not that the nomads "do" arithmetic or algebra, but because arithmetic and algebra arise in a strongly nomad-influenced world.

Up to now we have known three major types of human organization: *lineal, territorial,* and *numerical.* Lineal organization allows us to define so-called primitive societies. Clan lineages are essentially segments in action; they meld and divide, and vary according the ancestor considered, the tasks and the circumstances. Of course, number plays an important role in the determination of lineage, or in the creation of new lineages. As does the earth, since a clan segmentarity is doubled by a tribal segmentarity. The earth is before all else the matter upon which the dynamic of lineages is inscribed, and the number, a means of inscription: the lineages write upon the earth and with the number, constituting a kind of "geodesy".

Everything changes with State societies: it is often said that the territorial principle becomes dominant. One could also speak of deterritorialization, since the earth becomes an object, instead of being an active material element in combination with lineage. Property is precisely the deterritorialized relation between the human being and the earth: this is so whether property constitutes a good belonging to the State, superimposed upon continuing possession by a lineal community, or whether it itself becomes a good belonging to private individuals constituting a new community. In both cases (and according to the two poles of the State), something like an overcoding of the earth replaces geodesy. Of course, lineages remain very important, and numbers take on their own importance. But what moves to the forefront is a "territorial" organization, in the sense that all the segments, whether of lineage, land or number, are taken up by *an astronomical space or a geometrical extension* that overcodes them—but certainly not in the same way in the archaic imperial State and in modern States. The archaic State envelops a *spatium* with a summit, a differentiated space with depth and levels, while modern States (beginning with the Greek city-state) develop a homogeneous *extensio* with an immanent center, divisible homologous parts, and symmetrical and reversible relations. Not only do the two models, the astronomical and the geometrical, enter into intimate mixes; but even when they are supposedly pure, both imply the subordination of lineages and numbers to this metric power *(puissance)*, as it appears either in the *imperial spatium* or in the *political extensio.*[64] Arithmetic, the number, have always had a decisive role in the State apparatus: this is so even as early as the imperial bureaucracy, with the three con-joined operations of the census, taxation and election. It is even more true of modern forms of the State, which in developing utilized all the calculation techniques that were springing up at the border between mathematical science and social technology (there is a whole social calculus at the basis of political economy, demography, the organization of work, etc.). This arithmetic element of the State found its specific power in the treatment of all kinds of matter: primary matters (raw materials), the secondary matter of worked objects, or the ultimate matter constituted by the human population. Thus the number has always served to gain mastery over matter, to control its variations and movements, in other words to submit them to the spatio-temporal framework of the State—either the imperial *spatium*, or the modern *ex-tensio.*[65] The State has a territorial principle, or a princi-ple of deterritorialization, that links the number to metric magnitudes (taking into account the increasingly com-plex metrics operating the overcoding). We do not believe that the conditions of independence or autonomy of the Number are to be found in the State, even though all the factors of its development are present.

The *Numbering Number (Nombre nombrant)*, in other words autonomous arithmetic organization, implies neither a superior degree of abstraction nor very large quantities. It relates only to conditions of possibility constituted by nomadism, and to conditions of effectua-tion constituted by the war machine. It is in State armies that the problem of the treatment of large quantities arise, in relation to other matters; but the war machine

operates with small quantities that it treats using numbering numbers. These numbers appear as soon as one
distributes something in space, instead of dividing up
space or distributing space itself. The number becomes a
subject. The independence of the number in relation to
space is not a result of abstraction, but of the concrete
nature of smooth space, which is occupied without itself
being counted. The number is no longer a means of
counting or measuring, but of moving: it is the number
itself that moves through smooth space. There is undoubtedly a geometry of smooth space: but as we have
seen, it is a minor, operative geometry, a geometry of the
trait. The more independent space is from a metrics, the
more independent the number is from space. Geometry
as a royal science has little importance for the war
machine (its only importance is in State armies, and for
sedentary fortification, but it leads generals to serious
defeats[66]). The number becomes a principle whenever it
occupies a smooth space, and is deployed within it as
subject, instead of measuring a striated space. The number is the mobile occupant, the movable *(meuble)* in
smooth space, as opposed to the geometry of the immovable *(immeuble)* in striated space. The nomadic
numerical unit is the ambulant fire, and not the tent,
which is still too much of an immovable: "The fire takes
precedence over the yurt." The numbering number is no
longer subordinated to metric determinations or geometrical dimensions, but has only a dynamic relation
with geographical directions: it is a directional number,
not a dimensional or metric one. Nomad organization is
indissolubly arithmetic and directional; quantity is everywhere, tens, hundreds, direction is everywhere, left,
right: the numerical chief is also the chief of the left or the

right.[67] The numbering number is rhythmic, not harmonic. It is not related to cadence or measure: it is only in State armies, and for reasons of discipline and show, that one marches in cadence; but autonomous numerical organization finds its meaning elsewhere, whenever it is necessary to establish an *order of displacement* on the steppe, the desert—at the point where the lineages of the forest dwellers and the figures of the State lose their relevance. "He moved with the random walk which made only those sounds natural to the desert. Nothing in his passage would (indicate) that human flesh moved there. It was a way of walking so deeply conditioned in him that he didn't need to think about it. The feet moved of themselves, no measurable rhythm to their pacing."[68] In the war machine and nomadic existence, the number is no longer numbered *(nombré)*, but becomes a Cipher *(Chiffre)*, and it is in this capacity that it constitutes the *"esprit de corps"* and invents the secret and its outgrowths (strategy, espionage, war ruses, ambush, diplomacy, etc.).

A ciphered, rhythmic, directional, autonomous, movable, numbering number: the war machine is like the necessary consequence of nomadic organization (Moses experienced it, with all its consequences). Some people nowadays are too eager to criticize this numerical organization, denouncing it as a military or even concentration-camp society where people are no longer anything more than deterritorialized "numbers" *(numéros)*. But that is false. Horror for horror, the numerical organization of people is certainly no crueler than the lineal or State organizations. Treating people like numbers is not necessarily worse than treating them like trees to prune, or geometrical figures to contour and model. Moreover, the use of the number as a numeral, as a statistical element, is proper to the numbered number of the State, not to the numbering number. And the world of the concentration camp operates as much by lineages and territories as by numeration. The question is not one of good or bad, but of specificity. The specificity of numerical organization comes from the nomadic mode of existence and the war machine function. The numbering number is distinct both from lineal codes and State overcoding. Arithmetic composition on the one hand selects, extracts from the lineages the elements that will enter into nomadism and the war machine, and on the other hand directs them against the State apparatus, opposing a machine and an existence to the State apparatus, tracing a deterritorialization that traverses both the lineal territorialities and the territory or deterritoriality of the State.

A first characteristic of the numbering, nomadic or war, number is that it is always complex, that is, articulated. A complex of numbers every time. It is exactly for this reason that it in no way implies large, homogenized quantities, like State numbers or the numbered number, but rather produces its effect of immensity by its fine articulation, in other words by its distribution of heterogeneity in a free space. Even State armies do not do away with this principle when they deal with large numbers (despite the predominance of "base" 10). The Roman legion was a number made up of numbers, articulated in such a way that the segments became mobile, and the figures geometrical, changing, transformational. The complex or articulated number does not only comprise men, but necessarily weapons, animals and vehicles. The arithmetic base unit is therefore a unit of assemblage: for example, man-horse-bow, 1X1X1, according to the formula that carried the Scythians to triumph; and the formula becomes more complicated to the extent that certain "weapons" assemble or articulate several men or animals, as in the case of the chariot with two horses and two men, one to drive the other to throw, $2X1X2=1$; or in the case of the famous two-handled shield of the hoplite reform, which soldered together human chains. However small the unit, it is articulated. The numbering number always has several bases at the same time. It is also necessary to take into account arithmetic relations that are external, yet still contained in the number, expressing the proportion of combatants among the members of a lineage or tribe, the role of reserves and stocks, the upkeep of people, things and animals. *Logistics* is the art of these external relations, which are no less a part of the war machine than the internal relations of *strategy,* in other words the composition of combat units in relation to one another. The two together constitute the science of the articulation of numbers of war. Every assemblage has this strategic aspect and this logistical aspect.

But the numbering number has a second, more secret, characteristic. Everywhere, the war machine displays a curious process of arithmetic replication or doubling, as if it operated along two nonsymmetrical and nonequal series. *On the one hand,* the lineages are indeed organized and reshuffled numerically; a numerical composition is superimposed upon the lineages in order to make the new principle prevail. But *on the other hand,* men are simultaneously extracted from each lineage to form a special numerical body—as if the new numerical composition of the lineage-body could not succeed without the constitution of a body proper to it *(corps propre),* itself numeri-

cal. We believe that this is not an accidental phenomenon, but an essential constituent of the war machine, a
necessary operation for the autonomy of the number: the
number of the body must have as its correlate a body of
the number, the number must be doubled according to
two complementary operations. For the social body to be
numerized, the number must form a special body. When
Genghis Khan undertook his great composition of the
steppe, he numerically organized the lineages, and the
fighters in each lineage, placing them under a cipher and a
chief (groups of ten with decurions, groups of one
hundred with centurions, groups of one thousand with
chiliarchs). But he also extracted from each arithmetized
lineage a small number of men who were to constitute his
personal guard, in other words a dynamic formation
comprising a staff, commissars, messengers and diplomats ("antrustions").[69] One is never without the other: a
double deterritorialization, the second of which is to a
higher power *(puissance)*. When Moses undertook his
great composition of the desert—where the influence he
felt from the nomads was necessarily stronger than that
of Yahweh—he took a census of each tribe and organized
them numerically; but he also decreed a law according to
which the firstborn of each tribe at that particular time
belonged by right to Yahweh; as these firstborn were
obviously still too young, their role in the Number was
transferred to a special tribe, that of the Levites, who
provided the body of the Number or the special guard of
the ark; and as the Levites were less numerous than the
new firstborn of the tribes taken together, the excess
firstborn had to be bought back by the tribes in the form
of taxes (bringing us back to a fundamental aspect of
logistics). The war machine would be unable to function

without this double series: it is necessary both that numerical composition replace lineal organization, and that it conjure away the territorial organization of the State. Power in the war machine is defined according to this double series: power is no longer based on segments and centers, on the potential resonance of centers and overcoding of segments, but on these relations internal to the Number and independent of quantity. Tensions or power struggles are also a result of this: between Moses' tribes and the Levites, between Genghis' "noyans" and "antrustions." This is not simply a protest on the part of the lineages, wishing to regain their former autonomy; nor is it the prefiguration of a struggle for control over a State apparatus: it is a tension inherent in the war machine, in its special power, and in the particular limitations placed on the power *(puissance)* of the "chief."

Thus numerical composition, or the numbering number, implies several operations: the arithmetization of the starting aggregates, or sets (the lineages); the union of the extracted subsets (the constitution of groups of ten, one hundred, etc.); the formation by substitution of another set in correspondence with the united set (the special body). It is this last operation that implies the most variety and originality in nomad existence. The same problem arises even in State armies, when the war machine is appropriated by the State. In effect, if the arithmetization of the social body has as its correlate the formation of a distinct special body, itself arithmetic, this special body may be constructed in several ways: 1) from a privileged lineage or tribe, the dominance of which subsequently takes on a new meaning (the case of Moses, with the Levites); 2) from representatives of each lineage, who subsequently serve also as hostages (the firstborn:

this would actually be the Asian case, or the case of Genghis); 3) from a totally different element, one exterior to the base society, slaves, foreigners or people of another religion (this was already the case as early as the Saxon regime, in which the king used Frankish slaves to compose his special body; but Islam is the prime example, even inspiring a specific sociological category, that of "military slavery": the Mameluks of Egypt, slaves from the steppe or the Caucasus who were purchased at a very early age by the sultan; or the Ottoman Janissaries, who came from Christian communities[70]).

Is this not the origin of an important theme, "the nomads as child-stealers"? It is easy to see, especially in the last example, how the special body is instituted as a element determinant of power in the war machine. The war machine and nomadic existence have to conjure away two things simultaneously: a return of the lineal aristocracy, but also the formation of imperial functionaries. What complicates everything is that the State itself has often been determined in such a way as to use slaves as high functionaries: as we shall see, the reasons this was done varied, and that although the two currents conjoined in armies, they came from two distinct sources. For the power of slaves, foreigners, or captives in a war machine of nomadic origin is very different from the power of lineal aristocracies, but also from that of State functionaries and bureaucrats. They are "commissars," emissaries, diplomats, spies, strategists and logisticians, sometimes smiths. They cannot be explained away as a "whim of the sultan." On the contrary, it is the possibility of the war chief having whims that is explained by the objective existence and necessity of this special numerical body, this Cipher that has value only in relation to a *nomos.* There is both a deterritorialization and a becoming proper to the war machine: the special body, in particular the slave-infidel-foreigner, is the one who *becomes* a soldier and believer while remaining deterritorialized in relation to the lineages and the State. You have to be born an infidel to become a believer, you have to be born a slave to become a soldier. Specific schools or institutions are needed for this purpose: the special body is an invention proper to the war machine, which States always use, adapting it so totally to their own ends that it becomes unrecognizable, or restituting it in bureaucratic staff form, or in the technocratic form of very special bodies, or in *"esprit de corps"* that serve the State as much as they resist it, or among the commissioners who double the State as much as they serve it.

It is true that the nomads have no history; they only have a geography. And the defeat of the nomads was such, so complete, that history is one with the triumph of States. We have witnessed, as a result, a generalized critique dismissing the nomads as incapable of any innovation, whether technological or metallurgical, political or metaphysical. Historians, bourgeois or Soviet (Grousset or Vladimirtsov), consider the nomads a pitiable segment of humanity that understands nothing: not technology, to which it supposedly remained indifferent; not agriculture, not the cities and States it destroyed or conquered. It is difficult to see, however, how the nomads could have triumphed in war if they did not possess strong metallurgical capabilities: the idea that the nomad received his technical weapons and political counseling from renegades from an imperial State is highly improbable. It is difficult to see how the nomads could have undertaken to destroy cities and States, except in the

name of a nomad organization and a war machine
defined not by ignorance, but by their positive characteristics, by their specific space, by a composition all their
own that broke with lineages and conjured away the
State-form. History has always dismissed the nomads.
Attempts have been made to apply a properly military
category to the war machine (that of "military democracy"), and a properly sedentary category to nomadism
(that of "feudalism"). But these two hypotheses presuppose a territorial principle: either that an imperial State
appropriates the war machine, distributing land to warriors as a benefit of their position (*cleroi* and false fiefs),
or that property, once it has become private, in itself
posits relations of dependence among the property own-
ers constituting the army (true fiefs and vassalage[71]). In
both cases, the number is subordinated to an "immobile"
fiscal organization, in order to establish which land can
be or has been ceded as well as to fix the taxes owed by
the beneficiaries themselves. There is no doubt that
nomad organization and the war machine deal with these
same problems, both at the level of land and that of
taxation (in which the nomadic warriors were great
innovators, despite what is said to the contrary). But they
invent a territoriality and a "movable" fiscal organization that testifies to the autonomy of a numerical principle: there can be a confusion or combination of the
systems, but the specificity of the nomadic system remains the subordination of land to numbers that are
displaced and deployed, and of taxation to relations
internal to those numbers; already with Moses, for
example, taxation played a role in the relation between
the numerical bodies and the special body of the number). In short, military democracy and feudalism, far

from explaining the numerical composition of the nomads, instead testifies to what may survive of it in
sedentary regimes.

*Proposition 7: Nomad existence has for "affects"
the weapons of a war machine.*

A distinction can always be made between weapons
and tools on the basis of their usage (destroying people or
producing goods). But although this extrinsic distinction
explains certain secondary adaptations of a technical
object, it does not preclude a general convertibility
between the two groups, to the extent that it seems very
difficult to propose an intrinsic difference between weapons and tools. The types of percussion, as defined by
André Leroi-Gourhan, are found on both sides. "For ages
on end agricultural implements and weapons of war must
have remained identical."[72] Some have spoken of an
"ecosystem," situated not only at the origin, in which
work tools and weapons of war exchange their determinations: it seems that the same *machinic phylum* traverses
both. And yet we have the feeling that there are many
internal differences, even if they are not intrinsic, in other
words logical or conceptual, and even if they remain
approximate.

As a first approximation, weapons have a privileged
relation with projection. Anything that throws or is
thrown is fundamentally a weapon, and propulsion is its
essential moment. The weapon is ballistic; the very
notion of the "problem" is related to the war machine.
The more mechanisms of projection a tool has, the more
it behaves like a weapon, potentially or simply meta-
phorically. In addition, tools are constantly compensat-

ing for the projective mechanisms they possess, or else they adapt them to other ends. It is true that missile weapons, in the strict sense, whether projected or projecting, are only one kind among others; but even hand-held weapons require a usage of the hand and arm different from that of tools, a projective usage exemplified in the martial arts. The tool, on the other hand, is much more introceptive, introjective: it prepares a matter from a distance, in order to bring it to a state of equilibrium or to appropriate it for a form of interiority. Action at a distance exists in both cases, but in one case it is centrifugal, in the other centripetal. One could also say that the tool encounters resistances, to be conquered or put to use, while the weapon has to do with counterattack, to be avoided or invented (the counter attack is in fact the precipitating and inventive factor in the war machine, to the extent that it is not simply reducible to a quantitative rivalry or a defensive parade).

Secondly, weapons and tools do not "tendentially" (approximately) have the same relation to movement, to speed. It is yet another essential contribution of Paul Virilio to have stressed this weapon-speed complementarity: the weapon invents speed, or the discovery of speed invents the weapon (the projective character of weapons being the result). The war machine releases a vector of speed so specific to it that it needs a special name; it is not only the power of destruction, but "dromocracy" (=*nomos*). Among other advantages, this idea articulates a new mode of distinction between the hunt and war. For it is not only certain that war does not derive from the hunt, but also that the hunt does not promote weapons: either war evolved in the sphere of indistinction and convertiblity between weapons and tools, or it used to its own advantage weapons already distinguished, already constituted. As Virilio says, war in no way appears when man applies to man the relation of the *hunter* to the animal, but on the contrary when he captures the force of the *hunted* animal and enters into an entirely new relation to man, that of war (enemy, no longer prey). It is therefore not suprising that the war machine was the invention of the animal-raising nomads: animal breeding and training are not to be confused either with the primitive hunt or with sedentary domestication, but are in point of fact the discovery of a projecting and projectile system. Rather than operating by blow-by-blow violence, or constituting a violence "once and for all," the war machine, with breeding and training, institutes an entire economy of violence, in other words a way of making violence durable, even unlimited. "Bloodletting, immediate killing, run contrary to the unlimited usage of violence, that is to its economy . . . *The economy of violence is not that of the hunter in the animal raiser, but that of the hunted animal.* In horse-back riding, one conserves the kinetic energy, the speed of the horse, and no longer its proteins (the motor, and no longer the flesh). . . . Whereas in the hunt the hunter's aim was to arrest the movement of wild animality through systematic slaughter, the animal breeder sets about conserving it, and, by means of training, the rider joins with this movement, orienting it and provoking its acceleration." The technological motor would develop this tendency further, but "horse-back riding was the first projector of the warrior, his first system of arms."[73] Whence becoming-animal in the war machine. Does this mean that the war machine did not exist before horse-back riding and the cavalry? That is not the issue. The

issue is that the war machine implies the release of a
Speed vector that becomes a free or independent variable;
this does not occur in the hunt, where speed is associated
primarily with the hunted animal. It is possible for this
race vector to be released in an infantry, without recourse
to horse-back riding; it is possible, moreover, for there to
be horse-back riding, but as a means of transportation or
even of portage having nothing to do with the free vector.
In any event, what the warrior borrows from the animal
is more the idea of the motor than the model of the prey.
He does not generalize the idea of the prey by applying it
to the enemy, he abstracts the idea of the motor, applying
it to himself.

Two objections immediately arise. According to the
first, the war machine possesses as much weight and
gravity as it does speed (the distinction between the heavy
and the light, the dissymmetry between defense and
attack, the opposition between rest and tension). But it
would be easy to demonstrate that phenomena of "tem-
porization," and even of immobility and catatonia, so
important in wars, relate in certain cases to a component
of pure speed. And the rest of the time, they relate to the
conditions under which State apparatuses appropriate
the war machine, notably by arranging a striated space
where opposing forces can come to an equilibrium. It
happens that speed becomes abstracted as the property of
a projectile, a bullet or artillery shell, which condemns
the weapon itself, and the soldier, to immobility (for
example, immobility in the First World War). But an
equilibrium of forces is a phenomenon of resistance,
whereas the counterattack implies a rush or change of
speed that breaks the equilibrium: it was the tank that
regrouped all of the operations in the speed-vector, and

recreated a smooth space for movement by uprooting men and arms.[74]

The opposite objection is more complex: it is that speed does indeed seem to be as much a part of the tool as of the weapon, and is no way specific to the war machine. The history of the motor is not only military. But perhaps there is too much of a tendency to think in terms of quantities of movement, instead of seeking qualitative models. The two ideal models of the motor are those of work and *free action*. Work is a motor cause that meets resistances, operates upon the exterior, is consumed and spent in its effect, and must be renewed from one moment to the next. Free action is also a motor cause, but one which has no resistance to overcome, operates only upon the mobile body itself, is not consumed in its effect and continues from one moment to the next. Whatever its measure or degree, speed is relative in the first case, absolute in the second (the idea of a *perpetuum mobile*). In work, what counts is the point of application of a resultant force exerted by the weight of a body considered as "one" (gravity), and the relative displacement of this point of application. In free action, what counts is the way in which the elements of the body escape gravitation to occupy absolutely a nonpunctuated space. Weapons and weapon handling seem to be linked to a free action model, and tools to a work model. Linear displacement, from one point to another, constitutes the relative movement of the tool, but it is the vortical occupation of a space that constitutes the absolute movement of the weapon. It is as though the weapon were moving, self-propelling, while the tool is moved. This link between tools and work remains obscured unless work receives the motor, or real, definition we have just given it. The tool does not define work; just the opposite. The tool presupposes work. It must be added that weapons, also, obviously imply a renewal of the cause, an expending or even disappearance in the effect, the encountering of external resistances, a displacement of force, etc. It would be futile to credit weapons with a magical power *(puissance)* in contrast to the constraints of tools: weapons and tools are subject to the same laws, which define, precisely, their common sphere. But the principle behind all technology is to demonstrate that a technical element remains abstract, entirely undetermined, as long as one does not relate it to an *assemblage* it presupposes. It is the machine that is primary in relation to the technical element: not the technical machine, itself a collection of elements, but the social or collective machine, the machinic assemblage that determines what is a technical element at a given moment, what is its usage, extension, comprehension, etc.

It is through the intermediary of assemblages that the *phylum* selects, qualifies and even invents the technical elements. Thus one cannot speak of weapons or tools before defining the constituent assemblages they presuppose and enter into. This is what we meant when we said that weapons and tools are not merely distinguished from one another in an extrinsic manner, and yet they have no distinctive intrinsic characteristics. They have internal (and not intrinsic) characteristics relating to the respective assemblages with which they are associated. What effectuates a free action model is not the weapons in themselves and in their physical aspect, but the "war machine" assemblage as the formal cause of the weapons. And what effectuates the work model is not the tools, but the "work machine" assemblage as the formal cause of the tools. When we say that the weapon is inseparable from a speed-vector, while the tool remains linked to conditions of gravity, we are claiming only to signal a difference between two types of assemblage, a distinction that holds even if in the assemblage proper to it the tool is abstractly "faster," and the weapon abstractly more "weighty." The tool is by essence tied to a genesis, a displacement and an expenditure of force whose laws reside in work, while the weapon concerns only the exercise or manifestation of force in space and time, in conformity with free action. The weapon does not fall from the sky, and obviously assumes production, displacement, expenditure and resistance. But this aspect relates to the common sphere of the weapon and the tool, and does not yet concern the specificity of the weapon, which only appears when force is considered in itself, when it is no longer linked to anything but the number, movement, space or time, or *when speed is added to displacement*.[75] Concretely, a weapon as such does not relate to the Work model, but to the Free Action model, with the assumption that the conditions of work are fulfilled elsewhere. In short, from the point of view of force, the tool is tied to a gravity-displacement, weight-height system; the weapon to a speed-*perpetuum mobile* system (it is in this sense that it can be said that speed in itself is a "weapons system").

The very general primacy of the collective and machinic assemblage over the technical element applies generally, for tools as for weapons. Weapons and tools are consequences, nothing but consequences. It has often been remarked that a weapon is nothing outside of the combat organization it is bound up with. For example, "hoplite" weapons only existed by virtue of the phalanx as a mutation of the war machine: the only new weapon at the time, the two-handled shield, was created by this assemblage; the other weapons were preexistent, but in other combinations where they had a different function, a different nature.[76] It is always the assemblage that constitutes the weapons system. The lance and the sword came into existence in the Bronze only by virtue of the man-horse assemblage, which caused a lengthening of the dagger and pike, and disqualified the first infantry weapons, the morning star and the battle-ax. The stirrup, in turn, occasioned a new figure of the man-horse assemblage, entailing a new type of lance and new weapons; and this man-horse-stirrup constellation is itself variable, and has different effects depending on whether it is bound up with the general conditions of nomadism, or readapted later on to the sedentary conditions of feudalism. The situation is exactly the same for the tool: once again, everything depends on an organization of work, and variable assemblages of man, animal and thing. Thus the heavy plow only exists as a specific tool in a constellation where "long open fields" predominate, where the horse tends to replace the ox as draft animal, where the land begins to undergo triennial rotation, and where the economy becomes communal. Beforehand, the heavy plow may well have existed, but on the margins of other assemblages that did not bring out its specificity, that left unexploited its differential character with the scratch-plow.[77]

Assemblages are passional, they are compositions of desire. Desire has nothing to do with a natural or spontaneous determination; there is no desire but assembling, assembled, engineered desire (*agençant, agencé, machiné*). The rationality, the efficiency of an assemblage does not exist without the passions that the assemblage puts into play, without the desires that constitute it as much as it constitutes them. Detienne has shown that the Greek phalanx was inseparable from a whole reversal of values, and from a passional mutation that drastically changed the relations between desire and the war machine. It is a case of man dismounting from the horse, and of the man-animal relation being replaced by a relation between men in an infantry assemblage that paves the way for the advent of the peasant-soldier, the citizen soldier: the entire Eros of war changes, a group homosexual Eros tends to replace the zoosexual Eros of the horseman. Undoubtedly, whenever a State appropriates the war machine, it tends to assimilate the education of the citizen to the training of the worker to the apprenticeship of the soldier. But if it is true that all assemblages are assemblages of desire, the question is to know whether the assemblages of war and work, considered in themselves, do not fundamentally mobilize passions of different orders. Passions are effectuations of desire that differ according to the assemblage: it is not the same justice, nor the same cruelty, the same pity, etc. The work regime is inseparable from an organization and a development of Form, corresponding to which is the formation of the subject. This is the passional regime of feeling as "the form of the worker." Feeling implies an evaluation of matter and its resistances, a direction *(sens)*, also "meaning" to form and its developments, an economy of force and its displacements, an entire gravity. But the regime of the war machine is on the contrary that of *affects*, which relate only to the moving body in itself, to speeds and compositions of speed among elements. Affect is the active discharge of emotion, the counterattack, whereas feeling is an always displaced, retarded, resisting emotion. Affects are projectiles just like weapons, while feelings are introceptive like tools. There is a relation between the affect and the weapon, as witnessed not only in mythology, but also in the *chanson de geste,* and the chivalric novel or novel of courtly love. Weapons are affects, and affects weapons.

From this standpoint, the most absolute immobility, pure catatonia, are a part of the speed-vector, are carried by this vector, which links the petrification of the act to the precipitation of movement. The knight sleeps on his mount, then departs like an arrow. Kleist is the author who best integrated these sudden catatonic fits, swoons, suspenses, with the utmost speeds of a war machine: he presents us with a becoming-weapon of the technical element simultaneous to a becoming-affect of the passional element (the Penthesileia equation). The martial arts have always subordinated weapons to speed, and above all to mental (absolute) speed; for this reason, they are also the arts of suspense and immobility. The affect passes through both extremes. Thus the martial arts do not adhere to a *code,* as an affair of the State, but follow *ways (voies),* which are so many paths of the affect; upon these ways, one learns to "unuse" *(se desservir de)* weapons as much as one learns to use them, as if the strength *(puissance)* and cultivation of the affect were the true goal of the assemblage, the weapon being only a provisory means. Learning to undo things, and to undo oneself, is proper to the war machine: the "not-doing" of the warrior, the undoing of the subject. A movement of decoding traverses the war machine, while overcoding solders the tool to an organization of work and of the State (the tool is never unlearned, one can only com-

pensate for its absence). It is true that the martial arts
continually invoke the center of gravity and the rules for
its displacement. That is because these ways are not the
ultimate ones. However far they go, they are still in the
domain of Being, and only translate absolute movements
of another nature into the common space—those ef-
fectuated in the Void, not in nothingness, but in the
smooth of the void where there is no longer any goal:
attacks, counterattacks and headlong plunges . . .[78]

Still from the standpoint of the assemblage, there is an
essential relation between tools and signs. That is because
the work model that defines the tool belongs to the State
apparatus. It has often been said that people in primitive
societies do not work strictly speaking, even if their
activities are very constrained and regulated; and neither
does the man of war as such (the "labors" of Hercules
assume submission to a king). The technical element
becomes a tool when it is abstracted from the territory
and is applied to the earth as an object; but at the same
time, the sign ceases to be inscribed upon the body, and is
written upon an immobile, objective matter. For there to
be work, there must be a capture of activity by the State
apparatus, and a semiotization of activity by writing.
Whence the affinity between the assemblages signs-tools,
and signs of writing-organization of work. Entirely different is the case of the weapon, which is in an essential
relation with jewelry. Jewelry has undergone so many
secondary adaptations that we no longer have a clear
understanding of what it is. But something lights up in
our mind when we are told that metalworking was the
"barbarian," or nomad, art *par excellence,* and when we
see these masterpieces of minor art. These fibulas, these
gold or silver plaques, these pieces of jewelry, concern

small movable objects which are not only easy to transport, but which pertain to the object only as object in motion. These plaques constitute traits of expression of pure speed, carried on objects that are themselves mobile and moving. They do not enter into a relation of form-matter, but one of motif-support, where the earth is no longer anything more than ground *(sol)*, where there is no longer even any ground at all, since the support is as mobile as the motif. They give colors the speed of light, turning gold to red and silver into a white light. They are attached to the horse's harness, the sheath of the sword, the warrior's garments, the handle of the weapon: they even decorate things used only once, such as an arrowhead. Regardless of the effort or toil they imply, they are of the order of free action, related to pure mobility, and not of the order of work with its conditions of gravity, resistance and expenditure. The ambulant smith links metalworking to the weapon, and vice versa. Gold and silver have taken on many other functions, but cannot be understood apart from this nomadic contribution made by the war machine, in which they are not matters, but traits of expression appropriate to weapons (the whole mythology of war not only subsists in money, but is the active factor in it). Jewelry are the affects that correspond to weapons, that are swept up by the same speed-vector.

Metalworking, jewelry making, ornamentation, even decoration, do not form a writing, even though they have a power *(puissance)* of abstraction that is in every way equal to that of writing. Only this power is engineered *(agencé)* differently. In the case of writing, the nomads had no need to create their own system; they borrowed that of their sedentary imperial neighbors, who even furnished them with a phonetic transcription of their languages.[79] "Metalworking is the barbarian art *par excellence,* filigrees and gold or silver plating . . . Scythian art, linked to a nomadic and warlike economy that simultaneously made use of and rejected commerce (reserved for foreigners), was oriented towards this decorative and luxury aspect. The barabarians had no need to possess or create a specific code, for example an elementary picto-ideography, much less a syllabic writing system, which, moreover, would have been in competition with those used by their more advanced neighbors. In the fourth and third centuries B.C., the Scythian art of the Black Sea thus tended toward a graphic schematization of forms, which made it more a linear ornament than a proto-writing system."[80] Of course, one may write on jewelry, metal plaques, or even weapons; but only in the sense that one applies a preexisting writing system to these matters. The case of *runic writing* is more troubling, because its origins seem exclusively tied to jewelry, fibulas, elements of metalworking, small movable objects. The point is that in its early period runic writing had only a weak communication value, and a very restricted public function. Its secret character has led many to interpret it as magical writing. Rather, it is an affective semiotic, comprising in particular: 1) signatures, as marks of possession or fabrication; 2) short war or love messages. It constitutes a text that is "ornamental" rather than scriptural, "an invention with little utility, half-aborted," a substitute writing. It only takes on the value of writing during a second period, when monumental inscriptions appear, with the Danish reform of the ninth century A.D., in connection with the State and work.[81]

It may be objected that tools, weapons, signs and jewelry in fact occur everywhere, in a common sphere.

But that is not the problem, any more than it is to seek an origin in each case. It is a question of assigning assemblages, in other words of determining the *differential traits* according to which an element formally belongs to one assemblage rather than to another. It could also be said that architecture and cooking have an apparent affinity with the State, whereas music and drugs have differential traits which place them on the side of the nomadic war machine.[82] *It is therefore a differential method which establishes the distinction between weapons and tools,* from at least five points of view: the direction *(sens)* (projection-introception), the vector (speed-gravity), the model (free action-work), the expression (jewelry-signs), the passional or desiring tonality (affect-feeling). Doubtless the State apparatus tends to bring uniformity to the regimes, by disciplining its armies, by making work a fundamental unit, in other words by imposing its own traits. But it is not impossible for weapons and tools, if they are taken up by new assemblages of metamorphosis, to enter other relations of alliance. It happens that the man of war sometimes forms peasant or worker alliances, but it happens more often that a worker, industrial or agricultural, will reinvent a war machine. Peasants made an important contribution to the history of artillery during the Hussite wars, when Zisca armed mobile fortresses made from oxcarts with portable canons. A worker-soldier, weapon-tool, sentiment-affect affinity marks the right time, however fleeting, for revolutions and popular wars. There is a schizophrenic taste for the tool that moves it away from work and towards free action, a schizophrenic taste for the weapon that turns it into a means for peace, for obtaining peace. A counterattack and a resistance at the same time.

Everything is ambiguous. But we do not believe that Ernst Jünger's analyses are disqualified by this ambiguity, when he portrays the "Rebel" as a transhistorical figure drawing the Worker on the one hand, and the Soldier on the other, down a shared line of flight where one says simultaneously "I seek a weapon" and "I am looking for a tool": trace the line, or what amounts to the same thing, cross the line, pass over the line, for the line is only traced by surpassing the line of separation.[83] Undoubtedly, nothing is more outmoded than the man of war: he has long since been transformed into an entirely different character, the military man. And the worker himself has undergone so many misadventures . . .

And yet men of war reappear, with many ambiguities: they are all those who know the uselessness of violence, but who are adjacent to a war machine to be recreated, one of active, revolutionary counterattacks. Workers also reappear who do not believe in work, but who are adjacent to a work machine to be recreated, one of active resistance and technological liberation. They do not resuscitate old myths or archaic figures, they are the new figure of a transhistorical assemblage (neither historical, nor eternal, but untimely): the nomad warrior and the ambulant worker. A somber caricature already precedes them, the mercenary or mobile military instructor, and the technocrat or transhumant analyst, the CIA and IBM. But a transhistorical figure must defend himself as much against old myths as against preestablished, anticipatory disfigurations. "One does not go back to reconquer the myth, one encounters it anew, when time quakes at its foundations under the empire of extreme danger." Martial arts and state-of-the-art technologies only have value because they create a possibility of bringing together worker and warrior masses of a new type. The shared line of flight of the weapon and the tool: a pure possibility, a mutation. There arise subterranean, aerial, submarine technicians who belong more or less to the world order, but who involuntarily invent and amass virtual charges of knowledge and action that are usable by others, minute but easily acquired for new assemblages. The borrowings between warfare and the military apparatus, work and free action, always run in both directions, for a struggle that is all the more varied.

Problem 3: How do the nomads invent or find their weapons?

Proposition 8: Metallurgy in itself constitutes a flow necessarily confluent with nomadism.

The political, economic and social regime of the peoples of the steppe are less well known than their innovations in war, in the areas of offensive and defensive weapons, composition or strategy, and technological elements (the saddle, the stirrup, the horseshoe, the harness . . .). History contests each innovation, but cannot succeed in effacing the nomad traces. What the nomads invented was the man-animal-weapon, man-horse-bow assemblage. Through this assemblage of speed, the ages of metal are marked by innovation. The socketed bronze battle-ax of the Hyksos and the iron sword of the Hittites have been compared to miniature atomic bombs. It has been possible to establish a rather precise periodization of the weapons of the steppe, showing the alternation between heavy and light armament (the Scythian type and the Sarmatian type), and their mixed forms. The cast steel saber, often short and curved, a weapon for side attack with the edge of the blade, envelops a different dynamic space than the forged iron sword, for frontal attack using the point: it was the Scythians who brought it to India and Persia, where the Arabs would later acquire it. It is commonly agreed that the nomads lost their role as innovators with the advent of firearms, in particular the canon ("gunpowder got the better of their rapidity"). But it was not necessarily because they did not know how to use them: not only did armies like the Turkish army, whose nomadic traditions remained strong, develop extensive firepower, a new space; but additionally, and even more characteristically, light artillery was thoroughly integrated into mobile formations of wagons, pirate ships, etc. If the canon marks a limit for the nomads, it is on the contrary because it implies an economic investment that only a State apparatus can make (even commercial cities do not suffice). The fact remains that for weapons other than firearms, and also even for the canon, there is always a nomad to be seen on the horizon of a given *technological lineage*.[84]

Obviously, each case is controversial: the great discussions on the stirrup are an example.[85] The problem is that it is generally difficult to distinguish between what comes from the nomads as such, and what they receive from the empire with which they communicate, which they conquer or integrate with. There are so many gray areas, intermediaries and combinations between an imperial army and a nomad war machine that it is often the case that things come from the empire first. The example of the saber is typical, and unlike the stirrup, there is no longer any doubt: although it is true that the Scythians were the propagators of the saber, introducing it to the

Hindus, Persians, and Arabs, they were also its first
victims, they started off on the receiving end; it was
invented by the Chinese empire of the Ch'in and Han
Dynasties, the exclusive master of steel casting or crucible
steel.[86] This is a good example to use to bring out the
difficulties modern archeologists and historians have.
Even the archeologists are not immune from a certain
hatred or contempt for the nomads. In the case of the
saber, where the facts already speak sufficiently in favor
of an imperial origin, the best of the commentators finds
it fitting to add that the Scythians could not have invented
it at any rate—poor nomads that they were—and that
crucible steel necessarily came from a sedentary milieu.
But why follow the very old, official Chinese version
according to which deserters from the imperial army
revealed the secrets to the Scythians? And what can
"revealing the secret" mean if the Scythians were in
capable of putting it to use, and understood nothing of all
that? Blame the deserters, why don't you. You don't
make an atomic bomb with a secret, any more than you
make a saber if you are incapable of reproducing it, and
of integrating it under different conditions, of transfer-
ring it to other assemblages. Propagation, diffusion, are
fully a part of the line of innovation; they mark a bend in
it. On top of that: why say that crucible steel is necessarily
the property of sedentaries or imperial subjects, when it is
first of all the invention of metallurgists? It is assumed
that these metallurgists were necessarily controlled by a
State apparatus; but they also had to enjoy a certain
technological autonomy, and social clandestinity, which
means that, even controlled, they did not belong to the
State any more than they were themselves nomads. There
were no deserters who betrayed the secret, but rather

metallurgists who communicated it, and made its adaptation and propagation possible: an entirely different kind of "betrayal." In the last analysis, what makes the discussions so difficult (both in the controversial case of the stirrup and in the definite case of the saber) are not only the prejudices about the nomads, but also the absence of a sufficiently elaborated concept of the technological lineage (what defines a *technological line or continuum*, and its variable extension from this or that point of view?).

It would be useless to say that metallurgy is a science because it discovers constant laws, for example the melting point of a metal at all times and in all places. For metallurgy is inseparable from several lines of variation: variation between meteorites and indigenous metals; variation between ores and proportions of metal; variation between alloys, natural and artificial; variation between the operations performed upon a metal; variation between the qualities that make a given operation possible, or that results from a given operation. (For example, twelve varieties of copper identified and inventoried at Sumer by place of origin and degree of refinement.[87]) All of these variables can be grouped under two overall rubrics: *singularities or spatio-temporal haecceities* of different orders, and the operations associated with them as processes of deformation or transformation; *affective qualities or traits of expression* of different levels, which correspond to these singularities and operations (hardness, weight, color, etc.). Let us return to the example of the saber, or rather of crucible steel: it implies the actualization of a first singularity, namely the melting of the iron at high temperature; then a second singularity, the successive decarbonations; corresponding to these singularities are traits of expression—not only the hardness, sharpness, and finish, but also the undulations or designs traced by the crystallization and resulting from the internal structure of the cast steel. The iron sword is associated with entirely different singularities, since it is forged and not cast or molded, quenched and not air cooled, produced by the piece and not in number; its traits of expression are necessarily very different, because it pierces rather than hews, attacks from the front rather than from the side; and even the expressive designs are obtained in an entirely different way, by inlay.[88] We may speak of a *machinic phylum*, or technological lineage, wherever we find *a constellation of singularities, prolongable by certain operations, which converge, and make the operations converge, upon one or several assignable traits of expression.* If the singularities or operations diverge, in different materials or in the same material, we must distinguish two different phylums: this is precisely the case for the iron sword, descended from the dagger, and the steel saber, descended from the knife. Each phylum has its own singularities and operations, its own qualities and traits, which determine the relation of desire to the technical element (the affects that the saber "has" are not the same as those of the sword).

But it is always possible to situate the analysis on the level of singularities that are prolongable from one phylum to another, and to conjoin the two phylums. At the limit, . there is a single phylogenetic lineage, a single machinic phylum, ideally continuous: the flow of matter-movement, the flow of matter in continuous variation, conveying singularities and traits of expression. This operative and expressive flow is as much artificial as natural: it is like the unity of man and Nature. But at the same time, it is not realized in the here and now without dividing, differentiating. We will call an *assemblage* every constellation of singularities and traits deducted from the flow—selected, organized, stratified—in such a way as to converge (consistency) artificially and naturally: an assemblage, in this sense, is a veritable invention. Assemblages may group themselves into extremely vast constellations constituting "cultures," or even "ages"; within these constellations, the assemblages still differentiate the phylum or the flow, dividing it into so many different phylums, of a given order, on a given level, and introducing selective discontinuities in the ideal continuity of matter-movement. The assemblages cut the phylum up into distinct, differentiated lineages, at the same time as the machinic phylum cuts across them all, taking leave of one to pick up again in another, or making them coexist. A certain singularity embedded in the flanks of the phylum, for example the chemistry of carbon, will be brought up to the surface by a given assemblage that selects, organizes, invents it, and through which all or part of the phylum passes, at a given place at a given time. We may distinguish in every case a number of very different lines: some of them, phylogenetic lines, travel long distances between assemblages of various ages and cultures (from the blowgun to the canon? from the prayer wheel to the propeller? from the pot to the motor?); others, ontogenetic lines, are internal to one assemblage, and link up its various elements, or else cause one element to pass, often after a delay, into another assemblage of a different nature but of the same culture or age (for example, the horseshoe, which spread through agricultural assemblages). It is thus necessary to take into account the selective action of the assemblages upon the phylum, and the evolutionary reaction of the phylum as the subterranean thread which passes from one assemblage to another, or quits an assemblage, draws it forward and opens it up. *Vital impulse?* It is Leroi-Gourhan who has gone the farthest towards a technological vitalism taking biological evolution in general as the model for technical evolution: a *Universal Tendency*, laden with all of the singularities and traits of expression, traverses technical and interior milieus which refract or differentiate it in accordance with the singularities and traits each of them retains, selects, draws together, causes to converge, invents.[89] There is indeed a machinic phylum in variation which creates the technical assemblages, while the assemblages invent the various phylums. A technological lineage changes significantly according to whether one traces it upon the phylum or inscribes it in the assemblages; but the two are inseparable.

So how are we to define this matter-movement, this matter-energy, this matter-flow, this matter in variation which enters assemblages and leaves them? It is a destratified, deterritorialized matter. It seems to us that Husserl brought thought a decisive step forward when he discovered a region of *vague and material* essences (in other words essences that are vagabond, anexact and yet rigorous), distinguishing them from fixed, metric and formal, essences. We have seen that these vague essences are as distinct from formed things as they are from formal essences. They constitute fuzzy aggregates. They relate to a *corporeality (corporéité)* (materiality) that is not to be confused either with an intelligible, formal essentiality or a sensible, formed and perceived, thinghood *(choséité)*. This corporeality has two characteristics: on the one hand it is inseparable from passages to the limit as changes of state, from processes of deformation or transformation which operate in a space-time itself anexact and act in the manner of events (ablation, adjunction, projection . . .); on the other hand, it is inseparable from expressive or intensive qualities, which can be higher or lower in degree, and are produced in the manner of variable affects (resistance, hardness, weight, color . . .). There is thus an ambulant coupling, *events-affects*, which constitutes the vague corporeal essence, and is distinct from the sedentary linkage, "fixed essence-properties deriving therefrom in the thing." Doubtless Husserl had a tendency to make the vague essence a kind of intermediary between the essence and the sensible, between the thing and the concept, a little like the Kantian schema. Is not roundness a schematic or vague essence, intermediary between rounded sensible things and the conceptual essence of the circle? In effect, roundness exists only as an affect-threshold (neither flat nor pointed) and as a process-limit (becoming rounded), through sensible things and technical agents, millstone, lathe, wheel, spinning wheel, socket . . . But it is only "intermediary" to the extent that what is intermediary is autonomous, initially stretching *itself* between things, and between thoughts, to establish a whole new relation between thoughts and things, a *vague* identity between the two.

Certain distinctions proposed by Simondon can be compared to those of Husserl. For Simondon exposes the technological insufficiency of the matter-form model, in that it assumes a fixed form and a matter deemed homogeneous. It is the idea of the law that assures the model's coherence, since laws are what submit matter to this or that form, and, conversely, realize in matter a given property deduced from the form. But Simondon demonstrates that the *hylomorphic* model leaves many things, active and affective, by the wayside. On the one hand, to the formed or formable matter we must add an entire energetic materiality in movement, carrying *singularities or haecceities* that are already like implicit, topological rather than geometrical, forms, and which combine with processes of deformation: for example, the variable undulations and torsions of the fibers guiding the operation of splitting wood. On the other hand, to the essential properties of the matter deriving from the formal essence we must add *variable intensive affects*, now resulting from the operation, now on the contrary making it possible: for example, wood that is more or less porous, more or less elastic and resistant. At any rate, it is a question of surrendering to the wood, then of following where it leads by connecting operations to a materiality instead of imposing a form upon a matter: what one addresses is less a matter submitted to laws than a materiality possessing a *nomos*. One addresses less a form capable of imposing properties upon a matter than material traits of expression constituting affects. Of course, it is always possible to "translate" into a model that which escapes the model: thus, one may link the materiality's power *(puissance)* of variation to laws adapting a fixed form and a constant matter to one another. But this cannot be done without a distortion which consists in uprooting variables from their state of continuous variation, in order to extract from them fixed points and constant relations. Thus one throws the variables off, even changing the nature of the equations, which cease to be immanent to matter-movement (inequations, adequations). The question is not to know if such a translation is conceptually legitimate—it is—but only to know what intuition gets lost in it. In short, what Simondon criticizes the hylomorphic model for is taking form and matter to be two terms defined separately, like the ends of two half-chains whose connection can no longer be seen, like a simple relation of molding behind which there is a perpetually variable, continuous modulation that it is no longer possible to grasp.[90] The critique of the hylomorphic schema is based on "the existence, between form and matter, of a zone of medium and intermediary dimension," of energetic, molecular dimension—a space unto itself *(un espace propre)* that deploys its materiality through matter, a number unto itself *(un nombre propre)* that propels its traits through form . . .

We always get back to this definition: the *machinic phylum* is materiality, natural or artificial, and both simultaneously; it is matter in movement, in flux, in variation, matter as a conveyor of singularities and traits of expression. This has obvious consequences: namely, this matter-flow can only be *followed*. Doubtless, the operation which consists in following can be carried out in one place: an artisan who planes follows the wood, the fibers of the wood, without changing location. But this way of following is only one particular sequence in a more general process. For the artisan is obliged to follow in another way as well, in other words to go find the wood where it lies, and to find the wood with the right kind of fibers. Otherwise, he must have it brought to him: it is only because the merchant takes care of one segment of the journey in reverse that the artisan can avoid making the trip himself. But the artisan is complete only if he is also a prospector; and the organization that separates the prospector, the merchant and the artisan already mutilates the artisan in order to make a "worker" of him. We will therefore define the artisan as he who is determined in such a way as to follow a flow of matter, a *machinic phylum*. He is *the itinerant, the ambulant*. To follow the flow of matter is to itinerate, to ambulate. It is intuition in action. Of course, there are second-order itinerancies where it is no longer a flow of matter that one prospects and follows, but, for example, a market. Nevertheless, it is always a flow that is followed, even if the flow is not always that of matter. And, above all, there are secondary itinerancies: these are itinerancies which derive from another "condition," even if they are necessarily entailed by it. For example, a *transhumant*, whether a farmer or an animal raiser, changes land after it is worn out, or else seasonally; but he only secondarily follows a land flow, because he undertakes a rotation meant from the start to return him to the point from which he left, after the forest has regenerated, the land has rested, the weather has changed. The transhumant does not follow a flow, he traces a circuit; of the flow, he only follows that part which enters into the circuit, even an ever-widening one. The transhumant is therefore itinerant only consequentially, or becomes itinerant only when his circuit of land or pasture has been exhausted, or when the rotation has become so wide that the flows escape the circuit. Even the merchant is a transhumant, to the extent that mercantile flows are subordinated to the rotation between a point of departure and a point of arrival (go get-bring back, import-export, buy-sell). Whatever the reciprocal implications, there are considerable differences between a flow and a circuit. The *migrant*, we have seen, is something else again. And the *nomad* is not primarily defined as an *itinerant* or as a *transhumant*, nor as a *migrant*, even though he becomes these consequentially. The primary determination of the nomad is that he occupies and holds a smooth space: it is this aspect that determines him as nomad (essence). On his own account, he will be a transhumant, or an itinerant, only by virtue of the imperatives imposed by the smooth spaces. In short, whatever the de facto mixes between nomadism, itinerancy and transhumance, the primary concept is different in the three cases (smooth space, matter-flow, rotation). It is only on the basis of the distinct concept that we can make a judgment on the mix—on when it is produced, and on the form in which it is produced, and on the order in which it is produced.

But in the course of the preceding discussion, we have wandered from the question: why is the *machinic phylum*, the flow of matter, essentially metallic or metallurgical? Here again, it is only the distinct concept that can give us an answer, in that it shows that there is a special, primary relation between itinerance and metallurgy (deterritorialization). However, the examples we took from Husserl and Simondon concerned wood and clay as well as metals; and besides, are there not flows of grass, water, herds, which form so many phylums or matters in movement? It is easier for us to answer these questions now. For it is as if metal and metallurgy imposed upon and raised to consciousness something that is only hidden or buried in the other matters and operations. The difference is that elsewhere the operations take place between two thresholds, one of which constitutes the matter prepared for the operation, and the other the form to be incarnated (for example, the clay and the mold). The hylomorphic model derives its general value from this, since the incarnated form that marks the end of an operation can serve as the matter for a new operation, but in a fixed order marking a succession of thresholds. In metallurgy, on the other hand, the operations are always astride the thresholds, so that an energetic materiality overspills the prepared matter, and a qualitative deformation or transformation overspills the form.[91] For example, quenching follows forging and takes place after the form has been fixed. Or, to take another example, in molding, the metallurgist in a sense works inside the mold. Or again, steel that is melted and molded later undergoes a series of successive decarbonations. Finally, metallurgy has the option of melting down and reusing a matter to which it gives an *ingot-form*: the history of metal is inseparable from this very particular form, which is not to be confused with either a stock or a commodity; monetary value derives from it. More generally, the metallurgical idea of the "reducer" expresses this double liberation of a materiality in relation to a prepared matter, and of a transformation in relation to the form to be incarnated.

Matter and form have never seemed more rigid than in metallurgy; and yet the succession of forms tends to be replaced by the form of a continuous development, the variability of matters tends to be replaced by the matter of a continuous variation. If metallurgy has an essential relation with music, it is not only by virtue of the sounds of the forge, but of the tendency within both arts to bring into its own, beyond separate forms, a continuous development of form, and beyond variable matters, a continuous variation of matter: a widened chromaticism sustains both music and metallurgy; the musical smith was the first "transformer."[92] In short, what metal and metallurgy bring to light is a life inherent to matter, a vital state of matter as such, a material vitalism that doubtless exits everywhere but is ordinarily hidden or covered, rendered unrecognizable, dissociated by the hylomorphic model. Metallurgy is the consciousness or thought of the matter-flow, and metal the correlate of this consciousness. As expressed in panmetallism, metal is coextensive to the whole of matter, and the whole of matter to metallurgy. Even the waters, the grasses and varieties of wood, the animals are populated by salts or mineral elements. Not everything is metal, but metal is everywhere. Metal is the conductor of all matter. The machinic phylum is metallurgical, or at least has a metallic head, as its itinerant probe-head or guidance device. And thought is born more from metal than from stone: metallurgy is minor science in person, "vague" science or the phenomenology of matter. The prodigious idea of *Nonorganic Life*—the very same idea Worringer considered the barbarian idea *par excellence*[93]—was the invention, the intuition of metallurgy. Metal is neither a thing nor an organism, but a *body* without organs. The "Northern, or Gothic, line" is above all a mining or metallic line delimiting this body. The relation between metallurgy and alchemy does not, as Jung believed, repose on the symbolic value of metal and its correspondence with an organic soul, but on the immanent power *(puissance)* of corporeality in all matter, and on the *esprit de corps* accompanying it.

The first and primary itinerant is the artisan. But the artisan is neither the hunter, the farmer nor the animal raiser. Neither is he the winnower or the potter, who only secondarily take up craft activity. Rather, the artisan is he who follows the matter-flow as pure productivity: therefore in mineral form, and not in vegetable or animal form. He is not the man of the land, or of the soil, but of the subsoil. Metal is the pure productivity of matter, so he who follows metal is the producer of objects *par excellence*. As demonstrated by V. Gordon Childe, the metallurgist is the first specialized artisan, and in this respect forms a collective *body* (secret societies, guilds, journeymen's associations). The artisan-metallurgist is the itinerant, because he follows the matter-flow of the subsoil. Of course the metallurgist has relations with "the others," those of the soil, land and sky. He has relations with the farmers of the sedentary communities, and with the celestial functionaries of the empire who overcode those communities; in fact, he needs them to survive, he depends on an imperial agricultural stockpile for his very sustenance.[94] But in his work, he is in relation with the forest dwellers, and partially depends on them: he must establish his workshop near the forest, in order to obtain the necessary charcoal. In his space, he is in relation with the nomads, since the subsoil unites the ground *(sol)* of smooth space and the land of striated space: there are no mines in the alluvial valleys of the empire-dominated farmers, it is necessary to cross deserts, approach the mountains; and the question of control over the mines always involves nomadic peoples, *every mine is a line of flight* which is in communication with smooth spaces—today there are equivalents in the problems with oil.

Archaeology and history remain strangely silent on this question of the control over the mines. There have been empires with a strong metallurgical organization that had no mines; the Near East lacked tin, so necessary for the fabrication of bronze. Large quantities of metal arrived in ingot form, and from very far away (for instance, tin from Spain or even from Cornouaille). So complex a situation implies not only a strong imperial bureaucracy, and elaborate long-distance commercial circuits; it implies a shifting politics, in which States confront an outside, in which very different peoples confront one another, or else come to some accommodation particular aspects of the control of mines (extraction, charcoal, workshops, transportation). It is not enough to say that there are wars and mining expeditions; or to invoke "a Eurasian synthesis of the nomadic workshops from the approaches of China to the tip of Britanny," and remark that "the nomadic populations had been in contact with the principal metallurgical centers of the ancient world since prehistoric times."[95] What is needed is a better knowledge of the nomads' relations with these centers, with the smiths they themselves employed or frequented, with properly metallurgical peoples or groups who were their neighbors. What was the situation in the Caucasus and in the Altai? In Spain and North Africa? Mines are a source of flow, mixture and escape with few equivalents in history. Even when they are well controlled by an empire that owns them (the case of the Chinese Empire, the case of the Roman Empire), there is a major movement of clandestine exploitation, and of miners' alliances either with nomad and barbarian incursions or peasant revolts.

The study of myths, and even ethnographic considerations on the status of smiths, divert us from these political questions. Mythology and ethnology do not have the right method in this regard. It is too often asked how *the others* "react" to the smith: as a result, one succumbs to the usual platitudes about the ambivalence of *feelings*; it is said that the smith is simultaneously honored, feared and scorned—more or less scorned among the nomads, more or less honored among the sedentaries.[96] But this loses sight of the reasons for this situation, of the specificity of the smith himself, of the nonsymmetrical relation he entertains with the nomads and the sedentaries, the type of *affects* he invents (metallic affect). Before looking for the feelings of others toward the smith, it is necessary to evaluate the smith himself as an Other; as such, he has different affective relations with the sedentaries and the nomads.

There are no nomadic or sedentary smiths. The smith is ambulant, itinerant. Particularly important in this respect is the way in which the smith lives: his space is neither the striated space of the sedentary, nor the smooth space of the nomad. The smith may have a tent, he may have a house, he inhabits them in the manner of an "ore bed" *(gîte)* shelter, home, mineral deposit, like metal itself, in the manner of a cave or a hole, a hut half or all underground. They are cave-dwellers not by nature but by artistry and need.[97] A splendid text by Elie Faure evokes the infernal progress of the itinerant peoples of India as they bore holes in space and create the fantastic forms corresponding to these breakthroughs, the vital forms of nonorganic life: "There at the shore of the sea, at the base of a mountain, they encountered a great wall of granite. Then they all entered the granite; in its shadows they lived, loved, worked, died, were born, and, three or four centuries afterward, they came out again, leagues away, having traversed the mountain. Behind them they left the emptied rock, its galleries hollowed out in every direction, its sculptured, chiseled walls, its natural or artificial pillars turned into a deep lacework with ten thousand horrible or charming figures. . . . Here man confesses unresistingly his strength and his nothingness. He does not exact the affirmation of a determined ideal from form. . . . He extracts it rough from formlessness, according to the dictates of the formless. He utilizes the indentations and accidents of the rock. . . ."[98] Metallurgical India. Transpierce the mountains instead of scaling them, excavate the land instead of striating it, bore holes in space instead of keeping it smooth, turn the earth into swiss cheese. An image from the film *Strike* by Eisensteinpresents a holey space where a disturbing group of people are rising, each emerging from his hole as if from a field mined in all directions. The sign of Cain is the corporeal and affective sign of the subsoil, passing through both the striated land of sedentary space and the nomadic ground *(sol)* of smooth space without stopping at either one, the vagabond sign of itinerancy, the double theft and double betrayal of the metallurgist, who shuns agriculture at the same time as animal raising. Must we reserve the name Cainite for these metallurgical peoples who haunt the depths of History? Prehistoric Europe was crisscrossed by the *Battle-ax people*, who came in off the steppes like a detached metallic branch of the nomads, and the people known for their bell-shaped pottery, the *Beaker people*, originating in Andalusia, a detached branch of megalithic agriculture.[99] Strange peoples, dolicocephalics and brachycephalics who mix and spread across all of Europe. Are they the ones who kept up the mines, boring holes in European space from every direction, constituting our European space?

The smith is not nomadic among the nomads and sedentary among the sedentaries, nor half-nomadic among the nomads, half-sedentary among sedentaries. His relation to others results from his internal itinerancy, from his vague essence, and not the reverse. It is in his specificity, it is by virtue of his itinerancy, by virtue of his inventing a holey space, that he necessarily communicates with the sedentaries *and* with the nomads (and with others besides, with the transhumant forest dwellers). He is in himself double: a hybrid, an alloy, a twin formation. As Griaule says, the Dogon smith is not someone "impure," but "mixed," and it is because he is mixed that he is *endogamous*, that he does not intermarry with the pure, who have a simplified progeny while he reconstitutes a twin progeny.[100] Childe demonstrates that the metallurgist is necessarily doubled, that he exists two times, once as someone captured by and maintained within the apparatus of the Oriental empire, again in the Aegean world as someone much more mobile and much freer. *But the two segments cannot be separated*, simply by relating each of them to their particular context. The metallurgist belonging to an empire, the worker, presupposes a metallurgist-prospector, however far away; and the prospector ties in with a merchant, who brings the metal to the first metallurgist. In addition, the metal is worked on by each segment, and the ingot-form is common to them all: we must imagine less separate segments than a chain of mobile workshops constituting, from hole to hole, a line of variation, a gallery. Thus the relation of the metallurgist to the nomads and the sedentaries also passes via of the relations he has with other metallurgists.[101] This hybrid metallurgist, a weapon and tool maker, communicates with the sedentaries *and* with the nomads at the same time. Holey space itself communicates with smooth space and striated space. In effect, the machinic phylum or the metallic line passes through all of the assemblages: nothing is more deterritorialized than matter-movement. But it is not at all in the same way, and the two communications are not symmetrical. Worringer, in the domain of aesthetics, said that the abstract line took on two quite different expressions, one in barbarian Gothic art, the other in the organic Classical art. Here, we would say that the phylum simultaneously has two different modes of liaison: it is always *in connection* with nomad space, whereas it *conjugates* with sedentary space. On the side of the nomadic assemblages and war machines, it is a kind of rhizome, with its gaps, detours, subterranean passages, stems, openings, traits, holes, etc. On the other side, the sedentary assemblages and State apparatuses effect a capture of the phylum, put the traits of expression into a form or a code, make the holes resonate together, plug up the lines of flight, subordinate the technological operation to the work model, impose upon the connections a whole regime of arborescent conjunctions.

Axiom 3: The nomad war machine is the form of expression, of which itinerant metallurgy is the correlative form of content.

	Content	Expression
Substance	Holey Space (machinic phylum or matter-flow)	Smooth Space
Form	Itinerant Metallurgy	Nomad War Machine

Proposition 9: War does not necessarily have the battle as its object, and more importantly, the war

*machine does not necessarily have war as its object,
although war and the battle may be its necessary
result (under certain conditions).*

We now come to three successive problems: is the
battle the "object" of war? But also: is war the "object"
of the war machine? And finally, to what extent is the war
machine the "object" of the State apparatus? The ambiguity of the first two problems is certainly due to the term
object, but implies their dependency on the third. We
must nevertheless approach these problems gradually,
even if we are reduced to multiplying examples. The first
question, that of the battle, requires an immediate distinction to be made between two cases: when a battle is
sought, and when it is essentially avoided by the war
machine. These two cases in no way coincide with the
offensive and the defensive. But war in the strict sense
(according to a conception of it that culminated in Foch)
does seem to have the battle as its object, whereas guerilla
warfare explicitly aims for the *nonbattle*. However, the
development of war into the war of movement, and into
total war, also places the notion of the battle in question,
as much from the offensive as the defensive points of
view: the concept of the nonbattle seems capable of
expressing the speed of a flash attack, and the counter-
speed of an immediate response.[102] Conversely, the development of guerilla warfare implies a moment when, and
forms under which, a battle must be effectively sought, in
connection with exterior and interior "support points."
And it is true that guerilla warfare and war proper are
constantly borrowing each other's methods, and that the
borrowings run equally in both directions (for example,
stress has often been laid on the inspirations land-based

guerilla warfare received from maritime war). All we can say is that the battle and the nonbattle are the double object of war, according to a criterion that does not coincide with the offensive and the defensive, nor even with war proper and guerilla warfare.

That is why we push the question farther back, asking if war itself is the object of the war machine. It is not at all obvious. To the extent that war (with or without the battle) aims for the annihilation or capitulation of enemy forces, the war machine does not necessarily have war as it object (for example, the *raid* can be seen as another object, rather than as a particular form of war). But more generally, we have seen that the war machine was the invention of the nomad, because it is in its essence the constitutive element of smooth space, the occupation of this space, displacement within this space, and the corresponding composition of people: this is its sole and veritable positive object (*nomos*). Make the desert, the steppe, grow; do not depopulate it, quite the contrary. If war necessarily results, it is because the war machine collides with States and cities, as forces (of striation) opposing its positive object: from then on, the war machine has as its enemy the State, the city, the state and urban phenomenon, and adopts as its objective their annihilation. It is at this point that the war machine becomes war: annihilate the forces of the State, destroy the State-form. The Attila, or Genghis Khan, adventure clearly illustrates this progression from the positive object to the negative object. Speaking like Aristotle, we would say that war is neither the condition nor the object of the war machine, but necessarily accompanies or completes it; speaking like Derrida, we would say that war is the "supplement" of the war machine. It may even happen that this supplementarity is comprehended through a progressive, anxiety-ridden revelation. Such, for example, was the adventure of Moses: leaving the Egyptian State behind, launching into the desert, he begins by forming a war machine, on the inspiration of the old past of the nomadic Hebrews and on the advice of his father-in-law, who came from the nomads. This is the machine of the Just, already a war machine, but one that does not yet have war as its object. Moses realizes, little by little, in stages, that war is the necessary supplement of that machine, because it encounters or must cross cities and States, because it must send ahead spies (*armed observation*), then perhaps take things to extremes (*war of annihilation*). Then the Jewish people know doubt, and fear that they are not strong enough; but Moses also doubts, he shrinks before the revelation of this supplement. And it will be Joshua, not Moses, who is charged with waging war. Finally, speaking like Kant, we would say that the relation between war and the war machine is necessary, but "synthetic" (Yahweh is necessary for the synthesis).

The question of war, in turn, is pushed farther back, and is subordinated to the relations between the war machine and the State apparatus. States were not the first to make war: war, of course, is not a phenomenon one finds in the universality of Nature, as nonspecific violence. But war is not the object of States, quite the contrary. The most archaic States do not even seem to have had a war machine, and their domination, as we will see, was based on other agencies (comprising, rather, the police and prisons). It is safe to assume that the intervention of an extrinsic or nomad war machine that counterattacked and destroyed the archaic but powerful States was one of the mysterious reasons for their sudden annihilation. But the State learns fast. One of the biggest questions from the point of view of universal history is: how will the State *appropriate* the war machine, that is, constitute one for itself, in conformity with its size, its domination and its aims? And with what risks? (What we call a military institution, or army, is not at all the war machine in itself, but the form under which it is appropriated by the State.) In order to grasp the paradoxical character of such an undertaking, we must recapitulate the hypothesis in its entirety: 1) The war machine is that nomad invention which does not in fact have war as its primary object, but as its second-order, supplementary or synthetic objective, in the sense that it is determined in such way as to destroy the State-form and city-form with which it collides; 2) When the State appropriates the war machine, the latter obviously changes in nature and function, since it is afterward directed against the nomad and all State destroyers, or else expresses relations between States, to the extent that a State undertakes exclusively to destroy another State or impose its aims upon it; 3) It is precisely after the war machine has been appropriated by the State in this way that it tends to take war for its direct and primary object, for its "analytic" object (and that war tends to take the battle for its object). In short, it is at one and the same time that the State apparatus appropriates a war machine, that the war machine takes war as its object, and that war becomes subordinated to the aims of the State.

This question of appropriation is so varied historically that it is necessary to distinguish between several kinds of problems. The first concerns the possibility of the operation: it is precisely because war is only the supplementary or synthetic object of the nomad war machine that it experiences the hesitation that proves fatal to it, and that the State apparatus for its part is able to lay hold of war and thus turn the war machine back against the nomads. The hesitation of the nomad is legendary: what is to be done with the lands conquered and crossed? Return them to the desert, to the steppe, to open pastureland? Or let a State apparatus survive that is capable of exploiting them directly, at the risk of becoming, sooner or later, simply a new dynasty of that apparatus. Sooner or later, because Genghis Khan and his followers were able to hold out for a long time by partially integrating themselves into the conquered empires, while at the same time maintaining a smooth space on the steppes to which the imperial centers were subordinated. That was their genius, the *Pax Mongolica*. It remains the case that the integration of the nomads into the conquered empires was one of the most powerful factors of appropriation of the war machine by the State apparatus: the inevitable danger to which the nomads succombed. But there is another danger as well, the one threatening the State when it appropriates the war machine (all States have felt the weight of this danger, and the risks this appropriation represents for them). Tamerlane is the extreme example; he was not Genghis Khan's successor but his exact opposite: it was Tamerlane who constructed a fantastic war machine turned back against the nomads, but who, by that very fact, was obliged to erect a State apparatus all the heavier and more unproductive since it only existed as the empty form of appropriation of that machine.[103] Turning the war machine back against the nomads may constitute for the State a danger as great as that presented by nomads directing the war machine against States.

A second type of problem concerns the concrete forms the appropriation of the war machine takes: mercenary or territorial? A professional army or a conscripted army? A special body or national recruiting? Not only are these formulas not equivalent, but there are all the possible mixes between them. Perhaps the most relevant distinction to make, or the most general one, would be: is there merely "encastment" of the war machine, or "appropriation" proper? The capture of the war machine by the State apparatus took place following two paths, by encasting a society of warriors (who arrived from without or arose from within), or on the contrary by constituting it in accordance with rules corresponding to civil society whole. Once again, there is passage and transition from one formula to another. Lastly, the third type of problem concerns the means of appropriation. We must consider from this standpoint the various data pertaining to the fundamental aspects of the State apparatus: *territoriality, work or public works, taxation*. The constitution of a military institution or an army necessarily implies a territorialization of the war machine, in other words the granting of land ("colonial" or domestic), which can take very diverse forms. But at the same time, fiscal regimes determine both the nature of the services and taxes owed by the beneficiary warriors, and especially the kind of civil tax to which all or part of society is subject for the maintenance of the army. And the State enterprise of public works must be reorganized along the lines of a "laying out of the territory" in which the army plays a determining role, not only in the case of fortresses and fortified cities, but also in strategic communication, the logistical structure, the industrial infrastructure, etc. (the role and function of the Engineer in this form of appropriation[104]).

Let us compare this hypothesis as a whole with Clause-witz's formula: "War is the continuation of politics by other means." As we know, this formula is itself ex-tracted from a theoretical and practical, historic and transhistoric, whole *(ensemble)* the parts of which are interconnected: 1) There is a pure concept of war as absolute, unconditioned war, an Idea not given in experi-ence (bring down or "upset" the enemy, who is assumed to have no other determination, with no political, eco-nomic or social considerations entering in); 2) What is given are real wars as submitted to State aims; States are better or worse "conductors" in relation to absolute war, and in any case condition its realization in experience; 3) Real wars oscillate between two poles, both subject to State politics: the war of annihilation, which can escalate to total war (depending on what the objectives of the annihilation are), and tends to approach the uncon-ditioned concept via an ascent to extremes; and limited war, which is no "less" a war, but one that effects a descent towards limiting conditions, and can de-escalate to mere "armed observation."[105]

In the first place, the distinction between absolute war as Idea and real wars seems of great importance to us, but only with the possibility of applying a different criterion than that of Clausewitz. The pure Idea is not that of the abstract elimination of the adversary, but that of a war machine *which does not have war as its object*, and which only entertains a potential or supplementary synthetic relation with war. Thus the nomad war machine does not appear to us to be one case of real war among others, as in Clausewitz, but on the contrary the content adequate to the Idea, the invention of the Idea, with its own objects, space and composition of the *nomos*. Nevertheless it is still an Idea, and it is necessary to retain the concept of the pure Idea, even though this war machine was realized by the nomads. It is the nomads, rather, who remain an abstraction, an Idea, something real and nonactual, and for several reasons: first, because the elements of nomadism, as we have seen, enter into de facto mixes with elements of migration, itinerancy and tranhumance; this does not affect the purity of the concept, but introduces always mixed objects, or combinations of space and composition, which react back upon the war machine from the beginning. Second, even in the purity of its concept, the nomad war machine necessarily effectuates its synthetic relation with war as supplement, uncovered and developed in opposition to the State-form, the destruction of which is at issue. But that is exactly it; it does not effectuate this supplementary object or this synthetic relation without the State, for its part, finding the opportunity to appropriate the war machine, and the means of making war the direct object of this turned-around machine (thus the integration of the nomad into the State is a vector traversing nomadism from the very beginning, from the first act of war against the State).

The question is thus less that of the realization of war than of the appropriation of the war machine. It is at the same time that the State apparatus *appropriates* the war machine, subordinates it to its "political" *aims*, and gives it war as its direct *object*. And it is one and the same historical tendency that causes State to evolve from a triple point of view: going from figures of encastment to forms of appropriation proper, going from limited war to so-called total war, and transforming the relation between aim and object. The factors that make State war total war are closely connected to capitalism: it has to do with the investment of constant capital in equipment, industry and the war economy, and the investment of variable capital in the population in its physical and mental aspects (both as warmaker and victim of war[106]). Total war is not only a war of annihilation, but arises when annihilation takes as its "center" not only the enemy army, or the enemy State, but the entire population and its economy. The fact that this double investment can be made only under prior conditions of limited war illustrates the irresistible character of the capitalist tendency to develop total war.[107]

It is therefore true that total war remains subordinated to State political aims, and merely realizes the *maximal conditions* of the appropriation of the war machine by the State apparatus. But it is also true that when total war becomes the object of the appropriated war machine, then at this level of the set of all possible conditions, the object and the aim enter into new relations that can reach the point of contradiction. This explains Clausewitz's vacillation when he establishes at one point that total war remains a war conditioned by the political aim of States, and at another that it tends to effectuate the Idea of unconditioned war. In effect, the aim remains essentially political and determined as such by the State, but the object itself has become unlimited. We could say that the appropriation has changed direction, or rather that States tend to unleash, reconstitute, an immense war machine of which they are no longer anything more than the opposable or apposed parts. This worldwide war machine, which in a way "reissues" from the States, displays two successive figures: first, that of fascism, which makes war an unlimited movement with no other aim than itself; but fascism is only a rough sketch, and the second, post-fascist, figure is that of a war machine that takes peace as its object directly, as the peace of Terror or Survival. The war machine reforms a smooth space which now claims to control, to surround the entire earth. Total war itself is surpassed, towards a form of peace more terrifying still. The war machine has taken charge of the aim, worldwide order, and the States are no longer anything more than objects or means adapted to that machine. This is the point at which Clausewitz's formula is effectively reversed; to be entitled to say that politics is the continuation of war by other means, it is not enough to invert the order of the words as if they could be spoken in either direction; it is necessary to follow the real movement at the conclusion of which the States, having appropriated a war machine, and having adapted it to their aims, reissue a war machine that takes charge of the aim, appropriates the States and assumes increasingly wider political functions.[108]

Doubtless, the present situation is highly discouraging. We have watched the war machine grow stronger and stronger, as in a science fiction story; we have seen it assign as its objective a peace still more terrifying than fascist death; we have seen it maintain or instigate the most terrible of local wars as parts of itself; we have seen it set its sights on a new type of enemy, no longer another State, nor even another regime, but the "unspecified enemy"; we have seen it put its counter-guerilla elements into place, so that it can be caught by surprise once, but not twice . . . Yet the very conditions that make the State or World war machine possible, in other words constant capital (resources and equipment) and human variable capital, constantly recreate unexpected possibilities for counterattack, unforseen initiatives determining revolu-

tionary, popular, minority, mutant machines. The definition of the Unspecified Enemy testifies to this . . . "multi-
form, maneuvering and omnipresent . . . of the moral,
political, subversive or economic order, etc.," the unas-
signable material Saboteur or human Deserter assuming
the most diverse forms.[109] The first theoretical element of
importance is the fact that the war machine has many
varied meanings, and this is *precisely because the war
machine has an extremely variable relation to war itself.*
The war machine is not uniformly defined, and comprises
something other than increasing quantities of force. We
have tried to define two poles of the war machine: *at one
pole*, it takes war for its object, and forms a line of
destruction prolongable to the limits of the universe. But
in all of the shapes it assumes here—limited war, total
war, worldwide organization—war represents not at all
the supposed essence of the war machine, but only,
whatever the machine's power *(puissance)*, either the set
of conditions under which the States appropriate the
machine, even going so far as to project it as the horizon
of the world, or the dominant order of which the States
themselves are no longer but parts. *The other pole*
seemed to be the essence; it is when the war machine,
with infinitely lower "quantities," has as its object not
war, but the tracing of a creative line of flight, the
composition of a smooth space and of the movement of
people in that space. At this other pole, the machine does
indeed encounter war, but as its supplementary or synthetic object, now directed against the State and against
the worldwide axiomatic expressed by States.

We thought it possible to assign the invention of the
war machine to the nomads. This was done only in the
historical interest of demonstrating that the war machine

as such was invented, even if it displayed from the beginning all of the ambiguity which caused it to enter into composition with the other pole, and swing towards it from the start. However, in conformity with the essence, the nomads do not hold the secret: an "ideological," scientific or artistic movement can be a potential war machine, to the precise extent to which it traces, in relation to a *phylum*, a plane of consistency, a creative line of flight, a smooth space of displacement. It is not the nomad who defines this constellation of characteristics, it is this constellation which defines the nomad, and at the same time the essence of the war machine. If guerilla warfare, minority warfare, revolutionary and popular war, are in conformity with the essence, it is because they take war as an object all the more necessary for being merely "supplementary": *they can make war only on the condition that they simultaneously create something else*, if only new nonorganic social relations. The difference between the two poles is great, even, and especially, from the point of view of death: the line of flight that creates, *or* turns into a line of destruction; the plane of consistency that constitutes itself, even piece by piece, *or* turns into a plane of organization and domination. We are constantly reminded that there is communication between these two lines or planes, that each takes nourishment from the other, borrows from the other: the worst of the world war machines reconstitutes a smooth space to surround and enclose the earth. But the earth asserts its own powers *(puissances)* of deterritorialization, its lines of flight, its smooth spaces that live and blaze their way for a new earth. The question is not one of quantities, but of the incommensurable character of the quantities that confront one another in the two kinds of war machine, according to the two poles. War machines take shape against the apparatuses that appropriate the machine and make war their affair and their object: they bring connections to bear against the great conjunction of the apparatuses of capture or domination.

Notes

1. Georges Dumézil, *Mitra-Varuna* (Paris: Gallimard, 1948). On *nexum* and *mutuum*, the bond and the contract, see pp. 118-124.

2. "The first pole of the State (Varuna, Uranus, Romulus) operates by magic bond, seizure, or immediate capture: it does not wage battles, and has no war machine, it binds, and that is all." Its other pole (Mitra, Zeus, Numa) appropriates an army, but imposes upon it juridical and institutional rules which become nothing more than a piece of the State apparatus: thus Mars-Tiwaz is not a warrior god, but a god who is a "jurist of war." See Dumézil, *Mitra-Varuna*, pp. 113 ff., 148 ff., 202 ff.

3. Dumézil, *The Destiny of the Warrior*, trans. Alf Hiltebeital (Chicago: University of Chicago Press, 1970).

4. For the role of the warrior as one who "unties" and opposes both the magic bond and the juridical contract, see Dumézil, *Mitra-Varuna*, pp. 124-132. See also the analysis of *furor* in the works of Dumézil, passim.

5. TRANS: The first quote is from Friedrich Nietzsche, *The Genealogy of Morals*, Second Essay, Section 17, trans. Walter Kaufmann and R.J. Hollingdale (New York: Vintage, 1967), p. 86; the second is from Franz Kafka, "An Old Manuscript," *The Complete Stories* (New York: Schocken, 1983), p. 416.

6. Luc de Heusch emphasizes the public nature of Nkongolo's actions, in contrast to the secrecy of the actions of Mdibi and his son: in particular, the former eats in public, while the others hide during their meals. Later, we will see the essential relation of the war machine with the secret, which is as much a matter of principle as a result: espionage, strategy, diplomacy. Commentators have often underlined this link. *Le roi ivre ou l'origine de l'état* (Paris: Gallimard, 1972).

7. For an analysis of the three sins in the cases of the Indian

god Indra, the Scandinavian hero Starcatherus, and the Greek god Hercules, see Dumézil, *Mythe et épopée*, II, pp. 17-19 (Paris: Gallimard, 1971). See also Dumézil, *The Destiny of the Warrior*.

8. Dumézil, *Mitra-Varuna*, p. 135. Dumézil analyzes the dangers and causes of the confusion, which could be due to economic variables. See pp. 153, 159.

9. TRANS: *Richard III*, Act I, Scene i, line 158.

10. TRANS: See Clausewitz, *On War*, trans. Michael Howard, Peter Paret and Bernard Brodie (Princeton: Princeton University Press, 1976).

11. On Ajax and the tragedy of Sophocles, see the analysis of Jean Starobinski, *Trois Fureurs* (Paris: Gallimard, 1974). Starobinski explicitly raises the question of war and the State.

12. These themes are analyzed by Mathieu Carriére in an as yet unpublished study of Kleist.

13. Pierre Clastres, *Society Against the State*, trans. Robert Hurley (New York: Urizen, 1977), and "Archéologie de la violence: la guerre dans les sociétés primitives" and "Malheur du guerrier sauvage" in *Recherches d'anthropologie politique* (Paris: Seuil, 1980), pp. 171-208, 209-248. In the last text, Clastres paints the portrait of the destiny of the warrior in primitive society, and analyzes the mechanism which prevents the concentration of power (in the same way that Mauss demonstrated that the potlatch was a mechanism preventing the concentration of wealth).

14. Jacques Meunier, *Les gamins de Bogotá* (Paris: Lattès, 1977), p. 159 ("blackmail for dispersion") and p. 177: if necessary, "it is the other street childern who, by means of a complicated interplay of humiliations and silence, get the idea across that he must leave the gang." Meunier emphasizes the degree to which the fate of the ex-gang member is jeopardized: not only for health reasons, but because he finds it hard to integrate himself into the criminal underworld, a society too hierarchical, too cen-

tralized, too centered on organs of power for him to fit into (p. 178). On child gangs, see also the novel by Jorge Amado, *Capitâes de areia* (Sâo Paolo: Livraria Martins, 1944).

15. See I.S. Bernstein, "La dominance sociale chez les primates" in *La Recherche*, no. 91 (July, 1978).

16. Clastres, *Society Against the State*, p. 169: "The emergence of the State brought about the great typological division between Savage and Civilized man; it created the unbridgeable gulf whereby every thing was changed, for, on the other side, Time became History." In order to account for this emergence, Clastres cites first a demographic factor ("but there is no question of replacing an economic determinism with a demographic determinism," p. 180), then the possibility of a warring machine(?) running amok; he also cites, more unexpectedly, the indirect role of a certain mode of *prophetic speech*, which, at first directed against the "chiefs," produces a formidable new kind of power. But one obviously cannot prejudge more elaborated solutions Clastres might have found for this problem. On the possible role of prophetic speech, refer to Hélène Clastres, *La terre sans mal, le prophétisme tupi-guarani* (Paris: Editions du Seuil, 1975).

17. Michel Serres, *La naissance de la physique dans le texte de Lucrèce. Fleuves et turbulences* (Paris: Minuit, 1977). Serres was the first to make the three following points; the fourth seems to follow from them.

18. It is Pierre Boulez who makes this distinction between two kinds of space-time in music: in striated space, the measure can be irregular or regular, but it is always assignable; in smooth space, the partition, or break, "can be effected at will." *Boulez on Music Today*, trans. Susan Bradshaw and Richard Rodney Bennett (Cambridge, Mass.: Harvard University Press, 1971), p. 85.

19. Greek geometry is thoroughly marked by the opposition between these two poles, the theorematic and problematic,

and by the relative triumph of the former: Proclus, in his *Commentary of the First Book of Euclid's Elements* trans. and intro. Glenn R. Murrow (Princeton, N.J.: Princeton University Press, 1970) analyzes the difference between the poles, using as an example the Speusippus-Menaechmus opposition. Mathematics, also, has always been marked by this tension; for example, the axiomatic element has confronted a problematic, "intuitionist" or "constructivist" current emphasizing a calculus of problems very different from axiomatics, or any theorematic approach. See Georges Bouligand, *Le déclin des absolus mathématico-logiques* (Paris: Ed. d'Enseignement Supérieur, 1949).

20. Paul Virilio, *L'insécurité du territoire* (Paris: Stock, 1976), p. 120: "We know that the youth of geometry, geometry as free, creative investigation, came to an end with Archimedes. . . . The sword of a Roman soldier cut the thread, tradition says. In killing geometrical creation, the Roman State lay the foundation for the geometrical imperialism of the West."

21. With Monge, and especially Poncelet, the limits of sensible, or even spatial representation (striated space), are indeed surpassed, but less in the direction of a symbolic power *(puissance)* of abstraction than toward a transspatial imagination, or a transintuition (continuity). See Léon Brunschvicg's commentary on Poncelet, *Les étapes de la philosophie mathématique* (Paris: P.U.F., 1947).

22. Michel Serres (*La naissance de la physique*, pp. 105-107) analyzes the opposition d'Alembert-Bernoulli from this point of view. More generally, what is at issue is the difference between two models of space: "In the Mediterranean basin there is a shortage of water, and he who harnesses water rules. Hence that world of physics where the conduit is essential, and the *clinamen* seems like freedom because it is precisely that turbulence which rejects forced flow. Incomprehensible to scientific theory, incomprehensible to the master of the waters. . . . Hence the great

figure of Archimedes: the master of floating bodies and military machines" (p. 106).

23. See Benveniste, "The Notion of Rhythm in its Linguistic Expression" in *Problems in General Linguistics*, trans. Mary Elizabeth Meek (Coral Gables, Fla.: University of Miami Press, 1971), pp. 281-288. This text, often considered decisive, seems ambiguous to us because it invokes Democritus and atomism without dealing with the hydraulic question, and because it treats rhythm as a "secondary specialization" of the form of the body (p. 286).

24. Anne Querrien, *Devenir fonctionnaire ou le travail de l'Etat* (Paris: Cerfi). We have drawn from this book, as well as unpublished studies by Anne Querrien.

25. See Raoul Vergez, *Les illuminés de l'art royal. Huit siècles de compagnonnages* (Paris: Julliard, 1976), p. 54. TRANS: The word *trait*, which is central to Deleuze and Guattari's presentation, has a range of meanings not covered by any single word in English. Below, "trait" has been retained in the translation. The following connotations should be borne in mind. Literally, it refers to a graphic line, a stroke in a drawing or a set of strokes composing a drawing, the act of drawing a line. Abstractly, it is the purely graphic element. Figuratively, an identifying mark (a feature, or trait in the English sense), or any act constituting a mark or sign. It also refers to a projectile, especially an arrow, and to the act of throwing a projectile. In the present context, *trait* refers to the cutting-line followed by the artisan and to the working sketch of the construction under way. Vergez gives the following definition: "The Trait is a kind of graphic poem derived from geometry, which indicates the building plan in sketches traced with precision on the ground, showing sections, elevations and all other projections, the three dimensions of a volume," p. 86.

26. Gérard Desargues, *Oeuvres* (Paris: Leiber, 1864). See also the text by Michel Chasles, *Aperçu historique sur l'origine et le développement de méthodes en géométrie . . .* (Brus-

sels: M. Hayez, 1837) which establishes a continuity between Desargues, Monge and Poncelet as the "founders of a modern geometry."

27. Anne Querrien, *Devenir fonctionnaire*, pp. 26-27: "Is the State founded upon the collapse of experimentation?. . . . The State is not under construction, its construction sites must be short-lived. An installation is made to function, not to be socially constructed: from this point of view, the State only involves in the construction those who are payed to implement or command, and who are obliged to follow the model of a preestablished experimentation."

28. On the question of the "Colbert lobby," see Daniel Dessert and Jean-Louis Journet, "Le Lobby Colbert. Un royaume, ou une affaire de famille?" *Annales* 30, no. 6 (Nov.-Dec. 1975), 1303-1336.

29. See Ibn Khaldün, *The Muqaddimah: An Introduction to History*, tr. Franz Rosenthal (Princeton, N.J.: Princeton University Press, 1967). One of the essential themes of this masterpiece is the sociological problem of the *esprit de corps*, and its ambiguity. Ibn Khaldün contrasts bedouin existence (as a lifestyle, not as an ethnic group) with sedentary existence or city living. The first aspect of this oppostion is the inverted relation between the public and the secret: not only is there a secrecy of the bedouin war machine, as opposed to the publicity of the State city dweller, but in the first case "eminence" is based on a secret solidarity, while in the other case the secret is subordinated to the demands of social eminence. Second, bedouin existence brings into play both a great purity and a great mobility of the lineages and their genealogy, whereas city life makes for lineages that are very impure, and at the same time rigid and fixed: solidarity has a different meaning at each pole. Third, and this is the main point, bedouin lineages mobilize an *esprit de corps* and integrate into it, as a new dimension: this is *açabîyah*, or *ikhtilât*, from which the Arabic word for socialism is derived (Ibn Khaldün

stresses the absence of any "power" residing in the tribal chief, who has no State constraints at his disposal). On the other hand, in city living the *esprit de corps* becomes a dimension of power, and is adapted for "autocracy."

30. The principal texts of Husserl are *Ideas*, tr. W.R. Gibson (New York: Humanities Press, 1976), I,] 74, and *Edmund Husserl's Origin of Geometry: An Introduction*, tr. John P. Leavey, Jr., ed. David B. Allison (Stony Brook, NY: N. Hayes, 1978) (with Derrida's very important commentary, pp. 118-132). On the issue of a vague yet rigorous science, we may refer to the formula of Michel Serres, in his commentary on the geometrical figure called the *salinon*: "It is rigorous, anexact. And not precise, exact or inexact. Only a metrics is exact" (*Naissance de la physique*, p. 29). Gaston Bachelard's book, *Essai sur la connaissance approchée* (Paris: Vrin, 1927), remains the best study of the steps and procedures constituting a rigor of the anexact, and of their creative role in science.

31. Gilbert Simondon has contributed much to the analysis and critique of the hylomorphic schema, and of its social presuppositions ("form corresponds to what the man who commands has thought to himself, and must express in a positive manner when he gives his orders: form is thus of the order of the expressible"). To the form-matter schema, Simondon opposes a dynamic schema, that of matter endowed with singularities-forces, or the energetic conditions at the basis of a system. The result is an entirely different conception of the relations between science and technology. See *L'individu et sa genèse physico-biologique* (Paris: P.U.F., 1964).

32. In the text, *Timaeus*, 28-29, Plato entertains for an instant the thought that Becoming is not simply the inevitable characteristic of copies or reproductions, but could itself be a model rivalling the Identical and the Uniform. He only states this hypothesis in order to reject it; for it is true that if becoming is a model, then not only must the duality of the

model and the copy, of the model and reproduction, disappear, but the very notions of model and reproduction tend to lose all meaning. TRANS: Deleuze develops this point in "Plato and the Simulacrum," tr. Rosalind Krauss, *October* 27 (Winter 1983), pp. 45-56. See especially p. 53. (This essay appeared in French as an appendix to *Logique du sens*. Paris: Minuit, 1969, pp. 292-307).

33. TRANS: Friedrich Nietzsche, *The Will to Power*, tr. Walter Kaufmann (New York: Vintage, 1968),] 630 (1885), p. 336.

34. The situation is in fact more complex than that, and gravity is not the only feature of the dominant model: there is heat in addition to gravity (already in chemistry, combustion is coupled with weight). Even so, the problem was to know to what extent the "thermal field" deviated from gravitational space, or on the contrary was integrated with it. A typical example is that of Monge: he began by linking heat, light and electricity to the "variable affections of bodies," which would be the concern of "specific physics," while general physics would deal with extension, gravity, and movement. It was only later that Monge unified all of the fields under general physics (Anne Querrien).

35. Serres, *La naissance de la physique*, p. 65.

36. Carlos Castaneda, *The Teachings of Don Juan* (Berkeley, Ca.: University of California Press, 1971), p.88.

37. Albert Lautman has shown quite clearly how Riemann spaces, for example, admit a Euclidean conjunction such that it is possible at all times to define the parallelism of two neighboring vectors; this being the case, instead of exploring a multiplicity by legwork, the multiplicity is treated as though "immersed in a Euclidean space with a sufficient number of dimensions". See *Les schémas de structure* (Paris: Hermann, 1938), pp. 23-24, 43-47.

38. In Bergson, the relations between intuition and intelligence are very complex, they are in perpetual interaction. Bouligand's theme is also relevant here: the dualism of the two

mathematical elements, the "problem" and the "global synthesis," is only developed when they enter a field of interaction in which the global synthesis defines the "categories" without which the problem would have no general solution. See *Le déclin des absolus mathématico-logiques*.

39. Marcel Detienne, in *Les maîtres de vérité dans la Grèce archaïque* (Paris: Maspero, 1973), clearly articulates these two poles of thought, which correspond to the two aspects of sovereignty according to Dumézil: the magico-religious speech of the despot or of the "old man of the sea," and the dialogue-speech of the city. Not only are the principal character types of Greek thought (the Poet, the Physicist, the Philosopher, the Sophist . . .) situated in relation to these poles; but Detienne interposes between the two poles a distinct group, that of the Warriors, which assures transition or evolution.

40. There exists a Hegelianism of the right that lives on in official political philosophy, and weds the destiny of thought to the State. Alexandre Kojève, "Tyranny and Wisdom," in Leo Strauss, *On Tyranny* (New York: Free Press of Glencoe, 1963) and Eric Weil, *Hegel et l'Etat. Philosophie politique* (Paris: Vrin, 1974) are its recent representatives. From Hegel to Max Weber there developed a whole line of reflection on the relation of the modern State to Reason, both as rational-technical and as reasonable-human. If it is objected that this rationality, already present in the archaic imperial State, is the *optimum* of the governors themselves, the Hegelians respond that the rational-reasonable cannot exist without a minimum of participation by everybody. The question, rather, is whether the very form of the rational-reasonable is not extracted from the State, in a way that necessarily makes it right, gives it "reason" *(lui donner nécessairement "raison")*.

41. On the role of the ancient poet as a "functionary of sovereignty," See Dumézil, *Servius et la Fortune* (Paris:

Gallimard, 1943), pp. 64 ff., and Detienne, *Les maîtres de vérité*, pp. 17 ff.

42. See Michel Foucault's analysis of Maurice Blanchot and the form of exteriority of thought: "La pensée du dehors," *Critique*, no. 229 (June 1966), 523-548.

43. Nietzsche, *Schopenhauer as Educator*, in *Untimely Meditations*, tr. R.J. Hollingdale (New York: Cambridge University Press, 1983), pp. 177-178. and Malcolm Simpson (Chicago: Henry Regnery, Gateway Editions, 1965), pp. 84-85.

44. A curious text of Karl Jaspers, entitled *Descartes und die Philosophie* (Berlin: W. de Gruyter, 1956), develops this point of view, and accepts its implications.

45. Kenneth White, *Intellectual Nomadism*. The title of the second volume of this unpublished work is, precisely, *Poetry and Tribe*.

46. TRANS: Arthur Rimbaud, *A Season in Hell*, trans. Louise Varèse (Norfolk, CT: New Directions, 1952), pp. 9, 13, 17, 39.

47. Anny Milovanoff, "La seconde peau du nomade," *Nouvelles littéraires*, no. 2646 (27 July 1978), p. 18: "The Larbaâ nomads, on the border of the Algerian Sahara, use the word *trigâ*, which generally means road or way, to designate the woven straps serving to reinforce the cords holding the tent to the stakes. In nomad thought, the dwelling is not tied to a territory, but rather to an itinerary. Refusing to take possession of the land they cross, the nomads construct an environment out of wool and goat hair, one that leaves no mark at the temporary site it occupies. . . . Thus wool, a soft material, gives nomad life its unity. . . . Nomads pause at the representation of their journeys, not at a figuration of the space they cross. They leave space to space. . . . Woolly polymorphism."

48. See W. Montgomery Watt, *Mohammed at Medina* (London: Oxford University Press, 1956), pp. 85-86, 242.

49. Emmanuel Laroche, *Histoire de la racine "Nem" en grec*

ancien (Paris: Klincksieck, 1949). The root "Nem" indicates distribution, and not allocation, even when the two
are linked. In the pastoral sense, the distribution of animals
is effected in a nonlimited space, and implies no parcelling
out of land: "The occupation of shepherd, in the Homeric
age, had nothing to do with a parcelling of land; when the
agrarian question came to the foreground, in the time of
Solon, it was expressed in an entirely different vocabulary."
To take to pasture (nemô) does not refer to a parcelling out,
but to a scattering, to a repartition of animals. It was only
after Solon that Nomos came to designate the principle at
the basis of the laws and of right (Thesmoï and Dike), then
to be identified with the laws themselves. Prior to that,
there was instead an alternative between the city, or polis,
ruled by laws, and the outskirts as the place of the nomos. A
similar alternative is found in the work of Ibn Khaldün:
between *Hadara* as city living, and *Badiya* as nomos (not
the town, but the preurban countryside, the plateau,
steppe, mountain or desert).

50. Arnold Toynbee, *A Study of History* (New York: Oxford
University Press, 1947), abridged by D.C. Somerwell, Vol.
1, pp. 164-186: "They flung themselves upon the Steppe,
not to escape beyond its bounds but to make themselves at
home on it" (p. 168).

51. See Pierre Hubac, *Les nomades* (Paris: La Renaissance du
Livre, 1948), pp. 26-29 (although Hubac tends to confuse
nomads and migrants).

52. On the nomads of the sea, or of the archipelago, José
Emperaire writes: "They do not grasp an itinerary as a
whole, but in a fragmentary manner, by juxtaposing in
order its various successive stages, from campsite to campsite in the course of the journey. For each of these stages,
they estimate the length of the crossing and the successive
changes in direction marking it," *Les nomades de la mer*
(Paris: Gallimard, 1954), p. 225.

53. Wilfred Thesiger, *Arabian Sands* (London: Longmans,

Green & Co., 1959), pp. 112-113, 125, 165-166.

54. See the two admirable descriptions, of the sand desert by Wilfred Thesiger, above, and of the ice desert by Edmund Carpenter, *Eskimo* (Toronto: University of Toronto, 1964): the winds, and tactile and sound qualities; the secondary character of visual data, particularly the indifference of the nomads to astronomy as a royal science; and yet the presence of a whole minor science of qualitative variables and traces.

55. Emile Félix Gautier, *Le passé de l'Afrique du Nord* (Paris: Payot, 1952), pp. 267-316.

56. In this perspective, Clastres' analysis of Indian prophetism can be generalized: "On one side, the chiefs, on the other, and standing against them, the prophets ... And the prophetic machine worked perfectly well, since the *karai* were able to sweep astonishing masses of Indians along behind them ... the insurrectional act of the prophets against the chiefs conferred on the former, through a strange reversal of things, infinitely more power than was held by the latter," *Society Against the State*, pp. 184-185.

57. One of the most interesting themes of the classic work by Paul Alphandéry, *La chrétienité et l'idée de croisade* (Paris: Albin Michel, 1959), is his demonstration that the changes in course, the pauses, the detours were an integral part of the Crusade: "this army of crusaders that we envision as a modern army, like those of Louis XIV or Napoleon, marching with absolute passivity, obeying the will of a diplomatic officer and staff. Such an army knows where it is going, and when it makes a mistake, it is not for lack of reflection. A history more attentive to differences accepts a more realistic image of the army of the Crusade. The army of the Crusade was freely, sometimes anarchically alive. . . . This army was motivated from within, as a function of a complex coherence by virtue of which nothing happened by chance. It is certain that the conquest of Constantinople had its reason, necessity and a religious character, like the

other deeds of the Crusades" (Vol, 2, p. 7). Alphandéry shows in particular that the idea of a battle against the Infidel, *at any point*, appeared early, along with the idea of liberating the Holy Land (Vol 1, p. 219).

58. Modern historians have been inspired to fine analyses by this confrontation between the East and the West, which began in the Middle Ages (and is tied to the question: why did capitalism develop in the West and not elsewhere?). See especially Fernand Braudel, *Capitalism and Material Life, 1400-1800*, trans. Miriam Kochan (New York: Harper and Row, 1967), pp. 97-108; Pierre Chaunu, *L'expansion européenne du XIIIe au XVe siècle* (Paris: P.U.F., 1969), pp. 334-339 ("Why Europe? Why not China?"); Maurice Lombard, *Espaces et réseaux du haut Moyen Age* (The Hague: Mouton, 1971), chap. 8 (and p. 219: "What is called deforestation in the East is named clearing in the West. The first deep cause of the shift of the dominant centers from the East to the West is therefore a geographical reason: forest-clearing proved to have more potential than desert-oasis").

59. Marx's observations on the despotic formations of Asia have been confirmed by the African analyses of Max Gluckman, *Custom and Conflict in Africa* (Glencoe, Ill.: Free Press, 1959): at the same time immutability of form and constant rebellion. The idea of a "transformation" of the State indeed seems to be a Western one. And that other idea, the "destruction" of the State, belongs much more to the East, and to the conditions of a nomad war machine. Attempts have been made to present the two ideas as successive phases of revolution, but there are too many differences between them and they are difficult to reconcile; they reflect the opposition between the socialist and anarchist currents of the nineteenth century. The Western proletariat itself is perceived from two points of view: as having to seize power and transform the State apparatus (the point of view of labor-power *(force de travail)*, and as

willing or wishing for the destruction of the State (this time, the point of view of nomadization-power) *(force de nomadisation)*. Even Marx defines the proletariat as not only alienated (labor), but as deterritorialized. The proletariat, in this second perspective, appears as the heir to the nomad in the Western world. Not only did many anarchists invoke nomadic themes originating in the East, but the bourgeoisie above all were quick to equate proletarians and nomads, comparing Paris to a city haunted by nomads (see Louis Chevalier, *Laboring Classes and Dangerous Classes in Paris during the First Half of the Nineteenth Century*, trans., Frank Jellenck (New York: H. Fertig, 1973), pp. 362-366.

60. See Lucien Musset, *Les invasions. Le second assaut* (Paris: P.U.F., 1965): for example, the analysis of the Danes' three "phases," pp. 135-137).

61. Paul Virilio, *Vitesse et politique* (Paris: Galilée, 1977), pp. 21-22 and *passim*. Not only is the "town" unthinkable apart from the exterior flows with which it is in contact, and the circulation of which it regulates, but specific architectural aggregates, the fortress for example, are veritable transformers, by virtue of their interior spaces, which allow an analysis, prolongation or restitution of movement. Virilio concludes that the issue is less confinement than the management of the public ways, or the control of movement. Foucault was already moving in this direction with his analysis of the *naval hospital* as operator and filter: see *Discipline and Punish*, trans. Alan Sheridan (New York: Pantheon, 1977), pp. 143-146.

62. On Chinese, and Arab, navigation, the reasons behind their failure, and the importance of this question in the East-West "dossier", see Braudel, *Capitalism and Material Life*, pp. 300-309, and Chaunu, *L'expansion européenne*, pp. 145-147.

63. Virilio gives a very good definition of the *fleet in being* and its historical consequences: "The *fleet in being* is the

permanent presence at sea of an invisible fleet able to strike the adversary anywhere at any moment. . . . it is a new idea of violence which does not result from direct confrontation, but from the unequal properties of the bodies, from the evaluation of the quantities of movement permitted them in a chosen element, of the ongoing verification of their dynamic efficiency. . . . It is no longer a matter of crossing a continent, an ocean, from one town to another, from one shore to another; the *fleet in being* invents the notion of displacement without a destination in space and time. . . . The strategic submarine has no need to go anywhere in particular; all it must do, in holding the sea, is to remain invisible. . . . the realization of the absolute, uninterrupted circular voyage, for it.is without either departure or arrival. . . . If, as Lenin claimed, strategy is the choice of points for the application of force, we must conclude that these points today are no longer geo-strategic points of support, because starting from any point it is possible to reach any other point, wherever it is. . . . *Geographic localization* seems definitively to have lost its strategic value. Quite the opposite: this same value is attributed to the *delocalization of the vector*, the delocalization of a vector in permanent motion," *Vitesse et politique*, pp. 46-49, 132-133. The texts of Virilio are of great importance and originality in every respect. The only point that presents a difficulty for us is Virilio's assimilation of three groups of speed that seem very different to us: 1) speeds of nomadic, or revolutionary, tendency (riot, guerilla warfare); 2) speeds that are regulated, converted, appropriated by the State apparatus (management of the public ways); 3) speeds that are reinstated by a worldwide organization of total war, or planetary overarmament (from the *fleet in being* to nuclear strategy). Virilio tends to equate these groups on account of their interactions, and makes a general case for the "fascist" character of speed. It is, nevertheless, his own analyses that make these distinctions possible.

64. Jean-Pierre Vernant in particular has analyzed the connection between the Greek city-state and a homogeneous geometrical extension. *Mythe et pensée chez les Grecs* (Paris: Maspéro, 1971-1974), vol. 1, part 3. The problem is necessarily more complicated in relation to the archaic empires, or in relation to formations subsequent to the Classical city-state. That is because the space in question is very different. But it is still the case that the number is subordinated to space, as Vernant suggests with regard to Plato's ideal state. The Pythagorean or Neoplatonic conceptions of number envelop imperial astronomical spaces of a type other than homogeneous extension, but they maintain the subordination of the number: that is why Numbers become *ideal*, but not strictly speaking "numbering."

65. Dumézil stresses the role played by the arithmetic element in the earliest forms of political sovereignty. He even has a tendency to make it a third pole of sovereignty. See *Servius et la Fortune* and *Le troisième souverain* (Paris: Maisonneuve, 1949). But the role of this arithmetic element is, rather, to organize a matter; in so doing it submits that matter to one or the other of the two principal poles.

66. Carl von Clausewitz stresses the secondary role of geometry, in tactics and in strategy: *On War*, pp. 214-216 ("The Geometrical Factor").

67. See one of the most profound ancient texts relating the number and direction to the war machine, Ssu-ma Ch'ien, *The Records of the Grand Historian*, trans. Burton Watson (New York: Columbia University Press, 1961), Vol. 2, pp. 155-193 ("The Account of the Hsiung-nu").

68. Frank Herbert, *Children of Dune* (New York: Berkley Books, 1977), p. 212. One may refer to the characteristics proposed by Julia Kristeva to define the numbering number: "arrangement," "plural and contingent distribution," "infini-point," "rigorous approximation," etc. *Semeiotikè*.

Recherches pour une sémanalyse (Paris: Seuil, 1977), pp. 293-297.

69. Boris Iakovlevich Vladimirtsov, *Le régime social des Mongols*, tr. Michel Carsow (Paris: Maisonneuve, 1948). The term used by Vladimirtsov, "antrustions," is borrowed from the Saxon regime, in which the king's *company*, or "trust," was composed of Francs.

70. A particularly interesting case is that of a special body of smiths among the Tuaregs, called the *Enaden* (the "Others"); the Enaden are thought to have been originally Sudanese slaves, Jewish settlers in the Sahara, or descendents of the knights of Saint Louis. See René Pottier, "Les artisans sahariens du métal chez les Touareg," in *Techniques et civilisations*, Vol. 1 (Métaux et civilisations), no. 2 (1945), 31-40.

71. Feudalism is no less a military system than so-called military democracy; but the two systems presuppose an army integrated into some kind of State apparatus (for feudalism, it was the Carolingian land reform). It is Vladimirtsov who developed a feudal interpretation of the nomads of the steppe, while Mikhail Griaznov, *The Ancient Civilization of Southern Siberia*, tr. James Hogarth (New York: Cowles Book Co., 1969), leans toward military democracy. But one of Vladimirtsov's main arguments is that the organization of the nomads becomes feudal precisely to the extent that it is in disintegration, or is integrated into the empires it conquers. He himself remarks that in the beginning the Mongols did not organize the sedentary land they they took over into fiefs, true or false.

72. J.F.C. Fuller, *Armament and History* (New York: Charles Scribner's Sons: 1945), p. 5.

73. Paul Virilio, "Métempsychose du passager," *Traverses*, no. 8 (May 1977), 11-19. Virilio, however, asserts that there was an indirect transition from hunting to war: when women served as "portage or pack" animals, which already enabled the hunters to enter into a relation of "homosexual

duel" transcending the hunt. But it seems that Virilio himself invites us to make a distinction between *speed*, as projector and projectile, and *displacement*, as transport and portage. The war machine is defined from the first point of view, while the second relates to the public sphere. The horse, for example, is not a part of the war machine if it only serves to transport men who dismount to do battle. The war machine is defined by action, not transport, even if the transport reacts upon the action.

74. J.F.C. Fuller (*Armaments and History*, pp. 137 ff.) shows that the First World War was first conceived as an offensive war of movement based on artillery. But artillery was turned against artillery, forcing immobility. It was not possible to reinstate mobility in the war through "ever-increasing shell fire" (p. 138), since the craters made the terrain all the harder to negotiate. The solution, to which the English, and General Fuller in particular, made decisive contributions, came in the form of the tank: the tank, a "landship" (p. 139), reconstituted a kind of maritime or smooth space on land, and "superimposed naval tactics on land warfare" (p. 140). As a general rule, military response is never in kind: the tank was the response to artillery, the helicopter to the tank, etc. This makes for an innovation factor in the war machine that is very different from innovation in the work machine.

75. On this general distinction between the two models, "work-free action," "consuming force-conserving force," "real effect-formal effect," etc., see Martial Guéroult's exposition, *Dynamique et métaphysique leibniziennes* (Paris: Les Belles Lettres, 1934), pp. 55, 119 ff., 222-224.

76. Marcel Detienne, "La phalange, problèmes et controverses," in *Problèmes de la guerre en Grèce ancienne* (Civilisations et Sociétés, no. 11), ed. Jean-Pierre Vernant (The Hague: Mouton, 1968), pp. 119-143: "Technology is in a way internal to the social and the mental," p. 134.

77. On the stirrup and the plow, see Lynn Townsend White,

Jr., *Medieval Technology and Social Change* (New York: Oxford University Press, 1962), chapters 1 and 2. Similarly, it has been shown in the case of dry rice cultivation in Asia that the digging stick, the hoe and the plow depend upon collective assemblages which vary according to population density and the fallow period respectively. This enables Braudel to conclude: "The tool, according to this theory, is the result and no longer the cause" (*Capitalism and Material Life*, p. 116).

78. Treatises on martial arts remind us that the Ways, which are still subject to the laws of gravity, must be transcended in the void. Kleist's *About Marionettes* (trans. Michael Lebeck) (Mindelheim: Three Kings Press, 1970), without question one of the most spontaneously Oriental texts in Western literature, presents a similar movement: the linear displacement of the center of gravity is still "mechanical," and relates to something more "mysterious" that concerns the soul and knows nothing of weightiness.

79. See Paul Pelliot, "Les systèmes d'écriture en usage chez les anciens Mongols," *Asia Major*, 2 (1925), 284-289: the Mongols used the Uighur script, with the Syriac alphabet (it was the Tibetans who produced a phonetic theory of Uighur writing): the two versions of the *Secret History of the Mongols* that have been passed down to us are a Chinese translation and a phonetic transcription in Chinese characters.

80. Georges Charrière, *L'art barbare scythe* (Paris: Ed. du Cercle d'Art, 1971), p. 185.

81. See Lucien Musset, *Introduction à la runologie*, (Paris: Aubier-Montaigne, 1965).

82. There are, of course, forms of cooking and architecture that are part of the nomad war machine, but they fall under a different "trait," one distinguishing them from their sedentary form. Nomad architecture, for example the Eskimo igloo or the Hunnish wooden palace, is a derivative of the tent: its influence on sedentary art came by way of domes

and half-domes, and above all of *space starting very low*, as in a tent. As for nomad cooking, it consists literally of break-fast (the paschal tradition is nomadic). And it is under this trait that it can be part of a war machine: for example, the Janissaries had a cooking-pot as their rallying point, there were different ranks of cooks, and their hat had a wooden spoon through it.

83. It is in the *Traité du rebelle* (Paris: Bourgois, 1981) that Jünger takes his clearest stand against national socialism, and develops certain points contained in *Der Arbeiter*: a conception of the "line" as an active escape passing between the two figures of the old Soldier and the modern Worker, carrying both towards another destiny in another assembly (nothing of this remains in Heidegger's notion of the Line, although it is dedicated to Jünger).

84. Lynn White, who is actually not inclined to ascribe much power of innovation to the nomads, sometimes establishes extensive technological lineages with surprising origins: he traces hot air and turbine technologies to Malaya (*Medieval Technology and Social Change*, p. 95 and note): "Thus a chain of technological stimuli may be traced back from some of the major figures of early modern science and technology through the later Middle Ages to the jungles of Malaya. A second, and related, Malay invention, the fire piston, may have had significant influence upon the European understanding of air pressure and its applications."

85. On the particularly thorny question of the stirrup, see Lynn White, *Medieval Technology*, chap. 1.

86. See the fine article of A. Mazaheri, "Le sabre contre l'épée," *Annales*, 13, no.4 (October-December 1958), 669-686.

87. Henri Limet, *Le travail du métal au pays de Sumer au temps de la IIIe dynastie d'Ur* (Paris: Les Belles Lettres, 1960), pp. 33-40.

88. Along these lines, Mazaheri effectively demonstrates that the saber and sword belong to two distinct technological lineages. In particular, *damasking (damassage)*, which does

not come from Damascus at all, but rather from the Greek or Persian word for diamond, designates the treatment of cast steel that makes it as hard as a diamond, and the designs in this steel resulting from the crystallization of the cement ("true damask was made in the centers that had never experienced Roman domination"). But on the other hand, *damascening (damasquinage)*, which did come from Damascus, designates only inlay in metal (or in fabric), intentional designs imitating damasking using entirely different means.

89. André Leroi-Gourhan, *Milieu et techniques* (Paris: Albin Michel, 1945), pp. 356 ff. Gilbert Simondon, discussing short series, takes up the question of the "absolute origins of a technological lineage," or of the creation of a "technical essence": *Du mode d'existence des objects techniques* (Paris: Aubier, 1969), pp. 41-49.

90. On the mold-modulation relation, and the way in which molding hides or contracts an operation of modulation that is essential to matter-movement, see Simondon, *Du mode d'existence*, pp. 28-50 ("modulation is molding in a continuous and perpetually variable manner," p. 42). Simondon clearly shows that the hylomorphic schema owes its power not to the technological operation, but to the social model of *work* by which that operation is subsumed (pp. 47-49).

91. Simondon feels no special attraction for the problems of metallurgy. His analysis is not in fact historical, and prefers to deal with examples drawn from electronics. But, historically, there is no electronics without metallurgy. Thus Simondon pays hommage to metallurgy: "Metallurgy does not entirely accommodate itself to an analysis using the hylomorphic schema. The fixing of the form is not accomplished visibly in a single stroke, but in several successive operations; the forging and quenching of steel are anterior and posterior, respectively, to the fixing of the form in the strict sense; forging and quenching are, nevertheless, opera-

tions that constitute objects" (*L'individu*, p. 59).

92. Not only must myths be taken into account, but also positive history: for example, the role of "the brass" in the evolution of musical form; or again, the constitution of a "metallic synthesis" in electronic music (Richard Pinhas).

93. Wilhelm Worringer defines Gothic art in terms of a geometrical line that is "primitive," but has taken on life. But this vitality is not organic, as it will be in the Classical world: this line "embodies no organic expression. . . . it is nevertheless of the utmost vitality. . . . Since this line is lacking in all organic timbre, its expression of life must, as an expression, be divorced from organic life. . . . The pathos of movement which lies in this vitalized geometry— a prelude to the vitalized mathematics of Gothic architecture—forces our sensibility to an effort unnatural to it." *Form in Gothic* (London: Putnam's and Sons, 1927), pp. 41-42.

94. This is one of the essential points of V. Gordon Childe's argument in *The Prehistory of European Civilization* (London: Cassell and Co., 1962): the metallurgist is the first specialized artisan, whose sustenance is made possible by the formation of an agricultural surplus. The relation of the smith to agriculture has not only to do with the tools he manufactures, but also with the food he takes or receives. The Dogon myth, as analyzed in its variants by Griaule, can be seen as marking this relation, in which the smith receives or steals grains, and hides them in his mallet.

95. Maurice Lombard, *Les métaux dans l'ancien monde du Ve au XIe siècle* (Paris: Mouton, 1974), pp. 75, 255.

96. The social position of the smith has been the object of detailed studies, for Africa in particular: see the classic study by W.B. Cline, "Mining and Metallurgy in Negro Africa," *General Series in Anthropology*, no. 5 (1937); and Pierre Clément, "Le forgeron en Afrique noire," *Revue de géographie humaine et d'ethnologie* (1948). But these studies are hardly conclusive; the more well-defined the

principles invoked—"reaction of contempt," "of appro-
bation," "of apprehension"—the hazier and more over-
lapping the results, as witnessed by Clément's tables.

97. See Jules Bloch, *Les Tziganes*, Que sais-je?, no. 580 (Paris:
P.U.F., 1969). Bloch demonstrates precisely that the
distinction between sedentaries and nomads becomes
secondary in connection with cave dwelling.

98. Elie Faure, *Medieval Art*, Vol. 2 of *History of Art*, tr.
Walter Pach (Garden City, N.Y.: Garden City Publishing
Co., 1937), pp. 12-14.

99. On these peoples and their mysteries, see the analyses of
V. Gordon Childe, *The Prehistory of European Society*
(London: Cassell and Co., 1962), chap. 7 ("Missionaries,
Traders and Warriors of Temperate Europe"), and *The
Dawn of European Civilization* (New York: Knopf,
1958).

100. Maurice Griaule and Germaine Dieterlen, *Le renard pâle*,
Vol. 1 (Paris: Institut d'ethnologie, 1965), p. 376.

101. The book by Robert James Forbes, *Metallurgy in Anti-
quity* (Leiden: Brill, 1950), analyzes the different ages of
metallurgy, but also the types of metallurgist that existed
in the "ore stage": the "miner," who did the prospecting
and mining, the "smelter," who produced the crude metal
or alloy, the "blacksmith," who manufactured mass
products from crude metals, and the "metalworker," who
produced smaller objects; this includes gold- and silver-
smiths (pp. 74-76). The specialization system becomes
more complicated in the Iron Age, with attendant variations in the nomad-itinerant-sedentary distribution.

102. The texts of T.E. Lawrence, *Seven Pillars of Wisdom*
(New York: Doubleday, Doran and Co., 1935) and "The
Science of Guerilla War" in *Encyclopedia Britannica*,
14th ed. (1929), Vol 10, pp. 950-953, remain among the
most significant works on guerilla warfare; they present
themselves as an "anti-Foch" theory, and elaborate the
notion of the nonbattle. But the nonbattle has a history

that is not entirely dependent on guerilla warfare: 1) the traditional distinction between the "battle" and the "maneuver" in war. See Raymon Aron, *Penser la guerre. Clausewitz* (Paris: Gallimard, 1976), vol. 1, pp. 122-131; 2) the way in which the war of movement places the role and importance of the battle in question (as early as Marshal de Saxe, and the controversial question of the battle during the Napoleonic wars); 3) finally, more recently, the critique of the battle in the name of nuclear arms, which play a deterrent role, with conventional forces now having a role only in "testing" or "maneuver." See the Gaullist conception of the nonbattle, and Guy Brossollet, *Essai sur la non-bataille* (Paris: Belin, 1975)/. The recent return to the notion of the battle cannot be explained simply by technological factors such as the development of tactical nuclear arms, but implies political considerations—it is upon these that the role assigned to the battle (or nonbattle) in war depends.

103. On the fundamental differences between Tamerlane and Genghis Khan, see René Grousset, *The Empire of the Steppes*, trans. Naomi Walford (New Brunswick, N.J.: Rutgers University Press, 1970), pp. 417-419.

104. See *Armées et fiscalité dans le monde antique*, ed. A. Chastagnol, C. Nicolet, H. van Effenterre (Paris: C.N.R.S., 1977): this colloquim best covers the fiscal aspect, but deals with the other two as well. The question of the distribution of land to soldiers and the families of soldiers comes up in every State, and plays an essential role. In one particular form, it lay the foundation for fiefs and feudalism. But it already lay at the basis of "false fiefs" around the world, most notably of the *cleros* and cleruchy in Greek civilization. Claire Préaux, *L'économie royale des Lagides* (Brussels: Ed. de la Fondation Egyptologique Reine Elisabeth, 1939), pp. 463ff.

105. Clausewitz, *On War*, especially book 8, and the commentary of these three theses by Raymond Aron, *Penser la*

guerre, Vol. 1 (particularly pp. 139ff., "Pourquoi les guerres de la deuxième espèce?").

106. Erich Ludendorff, *Der totale krieg* (Munich: Ludendorff, Verlag, 1935) notes that the evolution has been toward attributing more and more importance to the "people" and "domestic policies" in war, whereas Clausewitz still puts the emphasis on armies and foreign policy. This criticism is true overall, despite certain texts of Clausewitz. The same criticism is also made by Lenin and the Marxists (although they obviously have a totally different conception of the people and domestic policy than Ludendorff). Certain authors have convincingly demonstrated that the proletariat is as much of military origin, naval in particular, as of industrial origin: for example, Virilio, *Vitesse et politique*, pp. 50-51, 86-87.

107. As John Ulric Nef shows, it was during the great period of "limited war" (1640-1740) that the phenomena of concentration, accumulation and investment occurred—the same phenomena that were later to determine "total war." See *War and Human Progress* (New York: Norton, 1968). The Napoleonic code of war represents a turning point that brought together the elements of total war: mobilization, transport, investment, information, etc.

108. On this "transcending" of fascism, and of total war; and on the new point of inversion of Clausewitz's formula, see Virilio's entire analysis in *L'insécurité du territoire*, especially chap. 1.

109. Guy Brossollet, *Essai sur la non-bataille*, pp. 15-16. The axiomatic notion of the "unspecified enemy" is already well-developed in official and unofficial texts on national defense, on international law and in the judicial or police spheres.

Demono

A STRATEGY GAME FOR TWO
PLAYERS DESIGNED BY P. M.
AUTHOR OF BOLO'BOLO AND
WELTGEIST SUPERSTAR

Who will win? The GREY world
of concrete, or the COLORED
world of Demons?

The GREY player wins by
profiting on an initial
credit. The COLORED player
wins by subverting
GREY's plans.

Please send me _____
DEMONO
@ $11.95 each

I enclose _____
the postage
is included

AUTONOMEDIA
BOX 568
BROOKLYN, N.Y. 1121

ABC

TRACKING THE SIGNIFIER
Theoretical Essays on Film, Linguistics, and Literature
Colin MacCabe

MacCabe is best known for his contributions to the British film studies journal *Screen* and for his role in the so-called "Cambridge structuralist controversy" of 1980-81. These essays date from the period that led to his departure from both *Screen* and Cambridge. Throughout, they reflect MacCabe's deep concern that the political implications of film, language, and literature not be lost or evaded. "This is an important book and a lively, entertaining, and provocative one."—Fredric Jameson
$27.50 cloth, $12.95 paper

DELIGHTFUL MURDER *A Social History of the Crime Story*
Ernest Mandel

Mandel shows how the crime story has reflected changes in bourgeois society and has served to reinforce the ideas that maintain the state's stability. His account ranges from the classics of Poe and Conan Doyle, Hammett and Chandler, to the spy stories of Maugham, Greene, and Ambler and modern novels like *Gorky Park*.
$19.50 cloth, $9.95 paper

New in the Theory and History of Literature series ———————
HETEROLOGIES *Discourse on the Other*
Michel de Certeau
Translated by **Brian Massumi.** Foreword by **Wlad Godzich.**

These essays illustrate the diversity of Certeau's concerns, which include psychoanalytic theory, historiography, and popular culture. His emphasis is on the fictive or literary aspects of discourse and on the ways disciplines define themselves and relate to one another. $29.50 cloth, $12.95 paper

JUST GAMING
Jean-François Lyotard and Jean-Loup Thébaud
Translated by **Wlad Godzich.** Afterword by **Samuel Weber,** translated by **Brian Massumi.**

In this dialogue on justice, the authors use Wittgenstein's theory of language games to examine the relationship of language to truth and the consequences for ethics and politics. Lyotard is the author of *The Postmodern Condition* and Thébaud the editor of *L'esprit.* $19.50 cloth, $9.95 paper

FRAMED NARRATIVES *Diderot's Genealogy of the Beholder*
Jay Caplan Afterword by **Jochen Schulte-Sasse**

Diderot's interpreters have approached the paradoxical nature of his work by imagining synthetic perspectives or frames within which the paradoxes could be resolved. Here Caplan focuses on the problem of framing *in* and *of* Diderot. He proposes an interpretive model that draws on Bakhtin's notion of dialogue, applying it to specific texts. $19.50 cloth, $9.95 paper

University of **Minnesota** *Press*
Minneapolis MN 55414

HORSEXE
ESSAY ON TRANSEXUALITY

CATHERINE MILLOT
Department of Psychoanalysis,
University of Paris, VIII

"Constantly open,
supple, nuanced,
analytic."
LE MONDE

"Finally, a psychoanalytic
study that reads like a
detective story...a
superb book on
the drama of man's
becoming woman."
MAGAZINE LITTÉRAIRE

Photo André Berg.

ISBN 0-936756-19-5 Cloth $19.95
ISBN 0-936756-20-9 Paper $8.95

From
the

POINT
HORS
LIGNE

**Psychoanalytic
Series**

Spring, 1986

AUTONOMEDIA
BOX 568
BROOKLYN, N.Y. 11211

semiotext(e), usa

A huge compendium of works in AMERICAN PSYCHO-TOPOGRAPHY — Areas not found on the official map of consensus perception — Maps of energies, secret maps of the USA in the form of words and images. Beyond instant-label left/right politics: Points where individualism and collectivism meet (or conflict in revealing ways) — Non-authoritarian, post-situationist, post-autonomist — Works based on consciousness and experience rather than ideology and abstraction — Involving real strategies (whether destructive or constructive) rather than only sterile critique and preaching. Turmoil. Guerrilla liaisons.

Distrust of all readymade categories (poetry, prose, graphics, essay, short story, criticism, socioanthropology, fiction, non-fiction). Instead, places where all these things coincide and so turn out to be SOMETHING ELSE — Hallucinatory advertisements — Essays in the form of comic strips, dada effusions, language subversions.

We are amazed. We are NOT BORED. We have discarded the outworn charm of post-modern incommunicadismo. Passion and involvement, self-abandoned craziness, funny, sexy, dangerous, unabashedly precious, punk, loud and direct. SF, speculative fiction, weird fantasy — Pornography — Other mutated genres — Sermons, rants, broadsheets, crackpot pamphlets, manifestoes — Xerox and mimeo zines — Punkzines — Mail art — Kids' poetry — Subverted advertisements — American samizdat — Astounding rhetoric, elegant propaganda — Underground comix — Geographical documentation (maps, monuments, guides to weird places, photographs) — Stolen top secret documents — And a special feature: scores of personal and classified ads, each one with a box-number or address, to connect YOU with the edges of the USA — anarchists, unidentified flying leftists, neo-pagans, secessionists, the lunatic fringe of survivalism, cults, foreign agents, mad bombers, ban-the-bombers, nudists, monarchists, children's liberation, tax resisters, zero-workers, mimeo poets, vampires, feuilletonistes, xerox pirates, prisoners, pataphysicians, unrepentant faggots, witches, hardcore youth, poetic terrorists...

**Edited by
Jim Fleming, SueAnn Harkey & Peter Lamborn Wilson**
$7.00 Each. Order from: Semiotext(E)

For the realization of almost-unheard-of desires

FOREIGN AGENTS SERIES

Jim Fleming and Sylvere Lotringer, Series Editors

SEMIOTEXT (E), 522 Philosophy Hall,
Columbia University, New York, NY 10027

Please send titles circled. I enclose $ _____ (include $1 postage)

SEMIOTEXT(E)

Subscription & Renewal Form

Please enter my subscription to **SEMIOTEXT(E)**
beginning with issue number ____

☐ New Subscription

☐ Renewal

Please Check One:
Subscription Rates (1 year/3 issues)

☐ Institution $24.00
☐ Regular $12.00
☐ Student $11.00

Foreign subscribers please add $3.00
for postage.

NAME _____

INSTITUTION (University, Library, Research Center) _____

ADDRESS _____

CITY _____ STATE _____ ZIP _____

COUNTRY _____ $ ____ enclosed